Software Leadership

Software Leadership
A Guide to Successful Software Development

Murray Cantor

✦ Addison-Wesley

Boston • San Francisco • New York • Toronto • Montreal
London • Munich • Paris • Madrid
Capetown • Sydney • Tokyo • Singapore • Mexico City

The publisher offers discounts on this book when ordered in quantity for special sales. For more information, please contact:

Pearson Education Corporate Sales Division
201 W. 103rd Street
Indianapolis, IN 46290
(800) 428-5331
corpsales@pearsoned.com

Visit us on the Web at www.awl.com/cseng/

Library of Congress Cataloging-in-Publication Data
Cantor, Murray, 1947-
    Software leadership : a guide to successful software development / Murray Cantor.
       p. cm.
    Includes bibliographical references and index.
    ISBN 0-201-70044-1 (alk. paper)
    I. Computer science—Development.   I. Title.

    QA76.76.D47 C364 2002
    005.1—dc21

                                                                2001046070

ISBN 0-201-70044-1
Text printed on recycled paper
1 2 3 4 5 6 7 8 9 10—CRS—0504030201
First printing, October 2001

Dedicated in the memory of my parents,
Joel and Muriel Cantor

Contents

Foreword xi

Preface xv

Introduction. xxi

Chapter 1   Quality Software 1

Product Stakeholders 4

Quality Attributes 13

What Price Quality? 23

The Zero-Defect Trap 24

The Bottom Line: Quality by Design 24

Chapter 2   Software Architecture 27

Architecture Defined 28

Specifying Software Architecture 29

Software Architecture 32

Quality Again 45

The Guiding Principle: Architecture First 49

Chapter 3   The Software Project 53

The Development Problem 54

Developing Products 55

Software Projects Are Nonlinear 58

Teams as Dynamic Nonlinear Systems 63
The Project Plan 66
Approaching Development Risk 67
A Word of Caution: No Silver Bullets 69

Chapter 4   Software Development Productivity 73
The Software Development Economics Model 74
Managing the Project Difficulty 76
Reducing the Size of the Effort 82
Improving the Efficiency of the Organization 86
Automating Routine Tasks 90
Round-Trip Engineering 93
The Road to Ruin: Misusing Overtime 94

Chapter 5   The Rational Unified Process 97
Adopt a Standard Process 98
Good and Bad Processes 99
Process Engineering 103
Iterative Development 103
The RUP Phases 104
Disciplines and Artifacts 111
Project Management 122
The Worst Thing You Can Do 123
The Reward: Improved Results 123

Chapter 6   Management and Leadership 127
Leadership Style 128
Team Leadership 131
Commitment and Buy-In 146
The Final Word: Modern Leadership 149

**Appendix   Three Failed Approaches to Software
                Development** 151
Some Misleading Analogies 152
The Waterfall Process 153

Hands-Off Approach 167
Rapid Prototyping 170
Industry Lessons Learned 173

Bibliography. 177
Index 183

Foreword

The *Dilbert* cartoon, by Scott Adams, features an amusing but hopelessly stupid character, called the "Pointy Hair Manager," who manages a department of a high-tech company. This gentleman's main characteristic, besides his hairdo, is that he seems to have absolutely no clue whatsoever as to what it is that his subordinates, like Dilbert, Alice, Wally, or Asok, are doing and what motivates them. Funny, outrageous, completely out of proportion? I am not so sure. Our industry is actually full of Pointy Hair Managers, with or without the hairdo; people who have been drawn, sometimes not of their own will, into managing "IT" (Information Technology) projects, or software development projects.

Are you a Pointy Hair Manager? Think again. Look in a mirror. You run the risk of finding a Dilbert cartoon taped on your door some day if you think that:

- software development is primarily about programming

- managing a software project is no different than managing any other project

- the best approach is to establish a detailed plan at the beginning and make sure everyone abides by it on a daily basis

- a safe way to proceed with the product is to freeze all requirements early in order to minimize any risk of schedule slippage and late surprises

- etc.

To really *manage*, as opposed to simply *administer*, good managers must understand the *nature* of what their team is producing, the dynamics of the team, the tools and processes they use, and all the risks associated with the development: anything that can hinder success. It happens that the very *nature of software* makes it somewhat different from other industrial endeavours, and simply transposing management techniques that work for, say, an engine or a bridge, will fail, or at least fail to deliver a quality product in the software domain.

Software differs from other products in several ways.

- It does not follow the "laws of physics," and the equivalent fundamental laws of software have not been discovered yet. This makes it difficult to accurately predict and plan without some form of experimentation or prototyping from which to get feedback.

- Software is essentially "soft," modifiable, and your external environment—customers, users—will expect your software to be changed, adapted, evolved, even as you develop it. Your management approach must acknowledge this.

- The techniques and tools used to design and build software evolve rapidly. These techniques have immense impact on software productivity, costs, risks, and quality—you must integrate them into your planning process.

- Software development costs are almost entirely engineering related. Since a software product can be "mass-produced" at very low cost, the economic model is very different from that of other manufactured goods.

These and other specificities of software make it more challenging for managers getting into software territory.

This book will help you *not* become a "Pointy Hair Manager." It will give you enough insight into the nature of software, the development process, and the techniques and tools used, so you can intelligently reason about the development, adjust, plan, re-plan, manage risks, and lead a team to success, not just document and record their failure.

I am delighted that our colleague Murray Cantor has chosen to base his new book on the Rational Unified Process. This will make it the book of choice for managers of teams using, or about to use, the Unified Process, in any of its variations, and who might be intimidated by the large amount of very technical material these processes contain. It will give them just enough knowledge about the

Unified Process to keep their "Dilberts" motivated, productive, and successful. But whatever process you ultimately decide to follow, you will find valuable guidance here for leading your team.

Happy reading! And best wishes for success in your next IT project.

Philippe Kruchten, Rational Fellow
Director of Process Development
Rational Software Corporation

Preface

I wrote this book mostly out of frustration. In my experience as a principal consultant in Rational Software's Strategic Services Organization, I find that software development is a dismal process for many organizations. Yet, from experience as a development manager and technical lead, I know it need not be so. In most instances, the problem may be traced to an inappropriate leadership approach. The frustration springs from knowing that this problem can be fixed.

Several books and articles focus on how badly software development is managed. It is not my intent to add to that literature, but to bring the reader the good news: Much has been learned about leading software organizations in the last four decades. By applying these lessons, the reader can become a much better leader (and follower) in any organization that develops software.

One reason I wrote this book is that I see an increasing need for software leadership skills. Not only is the software business continuing to grow, but also many firms in other sectors are coming to realize that an increasing amount of the value they deliver is in their software. Consider, for example, the design of medical ultrasound imaging machines, the instruments that are used to visualize fetuses in the womb. There are two design approaches:

- **Hardware-centric**—An old-line provider of medical instruments markets a piece of ultrasound equipment that is about the size of a writing desk and the weight of a small piano. It consists of a great deal of special hardware, not only to generate and receive the sound waves, but also to process the signals and generate the graphics. This instrument is expensive to manufacture and hard to maintain and upgrade.

- **Software-centric**—A small upstart competitor realized that it is possible to build an ultrasound imaging system out of off-the-shelf hardware: ASICs (programmable microchips), a Microsoft operating system, some transducers and receivers, liquid crystal displays, and the like. To bring an instrument to market, the upstart needed some industrial design to lay out the buttons and dials and to *create a great deal of proprietary software.* The upstart can bring a portable version, about 5.4 lb, to market for less than half the price of the old-line instrument and enjoy a large margin. If their software is well designed, their product will be more maintainable and expandable than the older system. The upstart's portable unit received government approval in March 1999 and in the first nine months of 2000 had revenues of $25M up from $745k from the previous year. They have not displaced the old-line company, but they have their attention. To stay competitive in medical instruments, the old-line instrument manufacturer finds itself in the software business.

This phenomenon is widespread—hardware firms increasingly realize that the value of their products is in their software. Automotive systems (all of those black boxes and engine controllers under the hood), telephone equipment (central office switches, cell phones), toys, entertainment devices, and almost everything else are affected by this phenomenon. I once had lunch with a manager of a division of a large tier-1 automobile parts supplier. His division makes automobile seats. I asked him to name his biggest problem. He answered it is the software that controls the high-end seats that is supposed to remember various driver preferences.

WHO SHOULD READ THIS BOOK

While writing the book, I had three kinds of readers in mind; each might approach the book differently:

- Line managers, especially those whose background is not in software development, but some other discipline such as engineering, product marketing, or general management

- Experienced software managers who are looking for more ways to make their organization more competitive

- Technical staff who are also leaders, interested in becoming leaders, or just in being led better

Readers with a technical background will gain a new perspective of a familiar landscape. They may gain a better idea of how to provide technical leadership and what to expect from their leaders. Line managers will gain new insights and perhaps find some new, more effective ways of providing leadership. Software project managers and team leaders may gain a new perspective on how to do their jobs better.

ROADMAP

The content of the book is based on the premise that a competent software development leader should have a good understanding of software quality, the most effective development practices, team dynamics, and the appropriate leadership style. Following that premise, I organized the book into the following sections.

- The Introduction provides background material on the state of the software development today and defines the success criteria for a software development effort.

- Chapter 1, Quality Software, provides a view of the product your team must develop and deliver. It contains insights into the attributes of quality software and introduces some steps you can take to make sure that quality is delivered. It discusses why delivering quality is both free and a matter of survival.

- Chapter 2, Software Architecture, is an overview of how software design is specified. It briefly describes the different views of software design, as well as their purposes and their roles in achieving quality. After reading this chapter, you will not be an architect, but you will be able to ask intelligent questions about architecture.

- Chapter 3, The Software Project, gives the big picture. It suggests that developing software is much like product development, and that much can be learned from that field's experience. This chapter provides an understanding of the problem-solving nature of the development project. Further, software development is inherently nonlinear, and this nonlinearity has profound implications for leading the project. The chapter delineates the key considerations of software leadership that are the framework for understanding the rest of the book.

- Chapter 4, Software Development Productivity, introduces a conceptual model of software productivity with three approaches for improving your organization's ability to deliver on its development commitments. The approaches form the basis of the modern software development practices discussed in Chapters 5 and 6.

- Chapter 5, The Rational Unified Process, introduces the modern best practices of software development project management. In addition, the chapter provides guidance on how to organize your software development projects. Chapter 5 explains how to determine the right amount of process and provides an important perspective on reuse.

- Chapter 6, Management and Leadership, describes the leadership style best suited in an organization that follows the principles and processes introduced in the earlier chapters. It explains the sort of leadership needed from the line and project managers. In particular, it describes the software development manager's role as an involved, constructive member of the development team. Making and meeting commitments in the face of uncertainty are explored.

- The appendix, Three Failed Approaches to Software Development, is based on industry experience. It provides a perspective on why many of the common approaches to software development fail and presents some important lessons on what not to do.

Throughout every chapter, there is a focus on the implications of the material to the leadership tasks.

Although I recommend everyone read all of the material, for some readers, some chapters will provide more value than others. Chapters 1 and 2 are about software itself. These chapters will be especially helpful to those who lack technical background. Chapters 3 through 5 provide an understanding of the development process. People familiar with the material in the earlier chapters but new to management will especially benefit from these chapters. However, this material will also be of use to many experienced managers who are interested in improving the competitive stance of their organization. Chapter 6 should be of interest to all readers.

Let me tell you about the appendix. I have decided to include this material in the hope many readers will recognize one or more of the errors in their own leadership approach and decide to try something different.

This book is intentionally brief, focusing on the big picture. A full treatment of many of the topics mentioned in the following chapters requires an entire separate book. To guide the reader who desires to learn more about the material, I provide an annotated listing of useful books and articles at the end of each chapter. There is also a combined bibliography at the end of the book.

ACKNOWLEDGMENTS

This book has benefited from the input of many colleagues: Some wittingly as reviewers, some just by sharing ideas in conversations. However, I especially want to thank Walker Royce, Philippe Krutchen, William Lochrie, Robert Brownsword, Michael Drexler, David Lubanko, and two anonymous reviewers for their frank and constructive comments on the earlier draft.

Introduction

This book is not about programming, object-oriented methodology, or even software project management. It is about leading an organization that performs these activities well. However, I will discuss those topics and others in passing, from a leadership perspective.

John P. Kotter, a leading expert in enterprise change, defines leadership as establishing direction, and aligning and motivating people. Management, on the other hand, consists of planning, organizing and staffing, and control and problem solving [Kotter, 1996]. Not every leader is a manager and vice versa. An appreciation of the management tasks is essential, but not sufficient to be an effective leader. This book touches on management to the extent necessary to provide a context for the discussion of leadership.

THE COMPETITIVE SOFTWARE ORGANIZATION

Software is a key asset for not only high-tech firms, but also old economy businesses. For example, one major automobile firm that deservedly has a good reputation for manufacturing quality vehicles is losing millions of dollars because of lack of good systems to track, forecast, and allocate cars once they leave the factory. Similarly, they are struggling with recovering warranty costs from their suppliers. If they could develop or acquire better software to support these functions, they would add a great deal to stockholder value.

Consider for a moment how the job of factory manager changed in the last century. In 1905, a manager might have hired the best craftsmen he could recruit and let them run the plant, checking periodically to see how things were going. By 1920, the manager would set up an assembly line process, hire unskilled workers to carry out very limited tasks, and run the line as fast as possible to maximize production. This manager relied on the process, not the skill of the workers. A modern factory manager needs to lead a team of highly professional specialists including manufacturing engineers, systems analysts, and operation researchers. He or she must understand the manufacturing, supply chain, configuration management, and inventory control processes as well as their automation, and how they are measured. He or she might review the measurements daily to detect changes in output volume or quality, call the appropriate department manager to find out the reason for the change, and take corrective action. Every month or so, the factory manager would review factory performance with his or her staff. The manager is expected to plan process improvements and track their status, communicating the status of the plans to upper management and staff regularly. In short, the manager is expected to apply a solid understanding of all the manufacturing processes, the tools used to automate them, and be able to provide effective leadership to highly technical staff.

Until recently, software development was much like manufacturing in 1905 or perhaps 1920. There was little automation. Some software managers hired the best craftsmen, divided the work, and hoped for the best. Many software organizations still operate this way. They put a positive spin on their approach by insisting that they "trust their people." Trusting people is essential, but it is not enough. Other managers set up a detailed process for dividing the work into a sequence of ordered steps. These managers hope that the process itself will provide the means for developing software. To them, once you understand the requirements, developing the software is a matter of connecting the dots. These managers constantly wonder why their projects are, in fact, so unpredictable. For reasons that I will explain in the text, although process is essential, it is not enough. It takes leadership for a team to develop software.

As a leader in a software development organization, you may not know how to write code, but you need to understand how your organization operates and you need to stay involved to lead your organization to success. The alternative, which involves betting your career on asking your people to deliver, then being disappointed when they "fail" you, is no way to live. It is better that you learn to be an expert in your role as a leader, working with people by understanding enough about what they are doing and the difficulties they face.

INVENTION ON A SCHEDULE

There are some compelling similarities between developing software and manufacturing hard goods. Both require

- Teams of specialists supported by automation tools

- Management discipline

- Effective leadership

The difference lies in the need for creativity. Developing software is sometimes described as invention on demand. The team must create a new program that meets some set of unique features on time and on budget.

Because of the need for creativity, the workflows and economic models of software development are markedly different from those of manufacturing or construction projects. In fact, software development shares some features with other disciplines that combine creativity with business discipline such as consumer product development or perhaps movie development. An excellent example can be found in Karl Sabbagh's text, *Twenty-First-Century Jet* (Scribner, 1966), which narrates the development of Boeing's 777 jetliner. The reader will find striking similarities of the airplane's design, not manufacture, with a software project.

The bar is set pretty high. Modern software development tools and processes enable the development of remarkably complex programs. Today, a program consisting of a million lines of code, new and reused, is not exceptional. Evidence of technically successful software developments surrounds us.

- The Internet, with its protocols, servers, and client applications

- Much of e-commerce

- The cellular telephone switches that keep track of calls as callers move from one cell to another

- The worldwide credit card transaction system

- The airlines reservation system

- All of the enterprise resource planning software running the back office operations of corporations, including inventory control and human resource management

- The embedded software in automobile engine controllers

- The CAD/CAM software that supported the paperless design of the Boeing 777

- The software that enables aerodynamically unstable military aircraft like the B2 to fly

- The space navigation systems that enable space probes to enter precise orbits of distant planets

- The computer animation software behind movies such as *Jurassic Park*, *Toy Story*, and *Dinosaur*

Further, these programs are being developed with unprecedented productivity. In the 1980s, it was common experience that the average programmer in a sizable project could create about 1,500–2,000 lines of tested code to the marketplace. Today, various case studies and personal experience show that ten times that productivity is possible.

The software development tools and processes that provide the opportunity to be more competitive are available to everyone. The difference is leadership.

THE SUCCESSFUL LEADER

This book is intended to provide the foundation that everyone needs to be a successful leader of a software developing organization. The first step is to understand the task:

A successful software organization makes and meets commitments to deliver quality software that meets stakeholders' needs within budget and on schedule.

This definition of success differs from some others. Some define project success as the delivery of the initially planned capability on the original schedule and budget. Our definition is more pragmatic: It is the outcome that matters, not adherence to a plan. The definition focuses on leading an organization whose projects have successful outcomes. When you deliver a system on time and on budget that meets customer needs and is adopted in the field, you will celebrate your team's success, and so will your management. The fact that the delivery will not include all the features on the initial list is of little concern, as long as management, the marketing and sales organizations, and the customers are not surprised.

To apply the definition, the leader must understand the stakeholders and their needs, the attributes of quality software, and how to enable the organization to achieve field success within the time and budget constraints. Further, the leader must understand how to deal with the inherent uncertainty facing any development requiring discovery of real users' needs and wants and invention to meet those needs.

LEADERSHIP IS KEY FOR MORALE

Good business and good works align at this junction. Maintaining a first-rate staff is critical to being competitive. In turn, retaining the best staff takes good leadership. On the other hand, poor leadership can result in low morale and eventual loss of key staff. I have been a software developer, a technical lead, a software architect, an architecture manager, a project manager, and a program manager. In my current job, I have the opportunity to assess many software organizations. Experience has led me to appreciate the harm done to people by poor software management. Developers are often stressed and depressed, feeling that much of their effort is wasted, their deadlines are without basis, and their managers do not have a clue as to what's going on. When describing their plight during project assessment interviews, developers sometimes yield to tears. This is unnecessary.

Software development need not be inhumane. I have shipped code in both commercial and contract settings. When the principles and techniques described in this book were applied, my teams achieved successful deliveries without experiencing the "death marches" and burnout still common in the industry.

PROFESSIONAL SATISFACTION

Leading an organization responsible for delivering software is often an unenviable position. This is especially true if the leader is unfamiliar with the principles necessary to manage a successful software development organization. He or she finds that the software is critical to company success, frequently on the critical path, and frequently late. The management may be panicking and the staff may be indignant. The leader reacts by reeling from crisis to crisis. Many managers even maintain two sets of books: one for reporting status to management, one for tracking real progress. None of this leads to job satisfaction or career enhancement. Again, it need not be so. With the background and techniques described in the book, the leader's days could be spent making good on commitments, enhancing his staff's quality of life, and building a competitive software organization. What could be more satisfying?

Chapter 1

Quality Software

To be a successful software leader, you need to understand the elements of software quality. This chapter provides a software quality framework by introducing the three product stakeholders: users, customers, and investors. This discussion is followed by a brief description of the different software quality parameters. A discussion of the cost and benefits of addressing quality ends the chapter.

The path to successful leadership starts with understanding the attributes of excellent software. Understanding quality software does not require that you learn programming. After all, you can be a successful factory manager without being a machinist. However, a successful factory manager does appreciate the product and the ways that the quality of the product can be evaluated.

As we will see, building quality code requires more than shipping thoroughly tested code. Quality, like beauty, is in the eye of the beholder. In the software world, the term for people who care about software quality, the beholders, is *stakeholders*. Different stakeholders have different quality concerns. Through understanding the needs of the different stakeholders you can understand the different dimensions of software quality. The following fictitious hardware example should help.

1.1 A CAUTIONARY PROBLEM

Imagine that you are in the business of developing and shipping laser printers for personal computers. Your marketing department says there is a market for a unit that prints 10 pages per minute and can be sold for less than $200. Your team is inexperienced, but dedicated. Through heroic efforts, they design and bring to market a printer that meets the performance and price goals. One way they meet the price goal is to have the factory solder the power supply directly to the other components rather than using a relatively expensive connector. The team uses a paper drive that is an older, less expensive model than those found in more expensive printers.

Your team is lauded for their efficient design. With much fanfare, your CEO tells the *Wall Street Journal* that this is the beginning of a new direction for the company. Even with the low price of the product, the investment in the printer development will be repaid with many years of follow-on products. The stock price goes up. You are proud of your team and their accomplishment, at least for a while.

After the product has been in the field a few weeks, the pain starts. Many machines begin to be returned, with three kinds of field problems.

- Customers who purchased the printer for their organization complain that printers do not work when delivered.

- Users are disappointed because the printer is slow.

- Users complain that the printer hangs up, or freezes, while printing certain pages and must be turned off and back on to function. The page during which the printer froze must be reprinted. Even worse, the purchasing departments report that organizations that adopt your printer have suffered a loss of productivity.

- Your company's service staff complains that the printers cannot be serviced in the field, causing a large number of returns.

You are puzzled by the problems. Your team tested the printers; they functioned properly and met performance specifications. You ask the marketing department to follow up with customers and suppliers to obtain more information. Inspections of the returns show that the solders connecting the power supply are failing because they are breaking during shipping. Your team works to develop alternatives. You are disappointed, but now that your team understands the problems, you are confident that they will soon be resolved.

The pain intensifies when the solder analysis team reports that there is no simple solution. Soldering is done in a factory overseas, and there is no straightforward way to improve the manufacturing quality. You cannot use connectors because there is no off-the-shelf connector and wiring harness available that can connect the power supply to the current design of the printer engine board, which was designed to accommodate solders, not connectors. You are faced with no good assembly alternatives, so the system must be redesigned.

Meanwhile, you turn your attention to the performance issue and the problem with the printer hanging up. Customers experiencing these problems are printing documents with a high percentage of graphics content. Your design team focused on printing fonts, creating special, fast font-rendering drivers. Unfortunately, the inexpensive EPROMs they chose to store the drivers do not allow for any acceleration in graphics rendering. Therefore, your machine prints any document with graphics more slowly than competing models. Even worse, the print processor's memory apparently becomes filled when printing some kinds of graphics, resulting in a system crash.

Your course of action is restricted to redesigning the board with more expensive volatile memory to hold graphics data and more expensive EPROMs to hold the graphics rendering code, which still needs to be developed. The bottom line is that in about a year you can deliver an acceptable printer that *misses* the price target. You do not relish explaining this to your management.

The final blow is a notice from Microsoft that they are revising their print driver specifications to take advantage of the accelerated Web document print performance they are planning. They intend to advertise this enhancement as a major advantage in their next operating system release; Web pages will print as fast as Microsoft Word™ documents. Manufacturers of printers that adopt the technology will be allowed to display a special logo: *WebPrint Inside*. The *WebPrint Inside* marketing program and the first supporting printers are expected to hit the market in six months. Your marketing consultants say that it is mandatory to have this logo to stay competitive. Your team says that to include this functionality, the software drivers would have to be completely redesigned, which would take 12 months, best case. They don't know how the competition does better.

You reach the inevitable conclusion that the product design is seriously flawed, and the product should be taken off the market. You must explain this to management, who must decide whether to abandon this business area. They have to explain to the analysts and the press why the investment in printer development was wasted. A good time is had by no one but the competition. Your stock price falls.

What went wrong?

The obvious answer is that the team made some unfortunate design decisions. Although the printer met requirements and passed system tests, it was not a quality product. It did not meet stakeholders' needs:

- The printer was too slow for many users.

- Customers found that the printer impeded their organization's productivity. The printer was not reliable; it failed frequently.

- The company management found their investment in the product did not pay off. The service costs eroded profits and the design provided no competitive advantage.

Briefly, the printer did not meet the needs of the intended users, customers, or investors. If the printer development manager had understood that quality includes meeting the needs of these stakeholders, this disaster might have been averted.

One more note. In the end, the element that defeated the printer was the inability of the embedded software to meet unexpected requirements, the *Web-Print Inside* functionality. No amount of compulsive up-front requirements analysis could have saved this product.

1.2 PRODUCT STAKEHOLDERS

There is more than one kind of stakeholder in software development. There are development stakeholders who are concerned about some aspect of the development process. An example of a *development stakeholder* is the testing organization. Those who have an interest in the quality of the finished product are called *product stakeholders*. They are the focus of this section.

Our printer example is applicable because it is useful to think of software as a product. As in any product development, there are three kinds of stakeholders with different but related concerns:

- *Users* of the software

- *Customers* who purchase and own the software license

- *Investors* who pay for the development and own the intellectual property

Note that any individual or organization could be more than one kind of stakeholder. A user could also be a customer, and a customer could be an investor. Consider some common cases:

- **Consumer software**—software such as computer games developed for retail sales. In this case, the users are likely to be the purchasers. The company that developed the software is the investor.

- **Enterprise software**—large systems designed to be purchased without modification by organizations. Examples include software for computer-aided design, or professional publishing systems. In this case, the customer is often some information technology organization, not the users of the software. The developing company is the investor.

- **Custom software**—systems developed on contract. Examples of contractors can include government agencies, or large private enterprises. For example, the Department of Defense may contract for mission planning software to be used by military officers, the users. A private sector example of a contractor is an airline wanting a new reservation system. In this case, the customer is usually a different organization than the user. Depending on the deal, the investor is either the developing company, the contracting company, or both.

- **Customized components**—proprietary systems consisting of reusable components that are installed with significant customization. Enterprise resource planners such as PeopleSoft fall in this category. The customers are the information technology departments of companies who deploy the software. The users are typically found in other departments. The investor is the developing company.

- **Embedded software**—the customers are manufacturers who intend to embed the software in their hardware or software products. Examples include automobile, consumer product, and toy companies. Their customers are the users.

To be able to deliver quality software for such a wide variety of cases, one must understand the stakeholders and how to meet their needs. The remainder of this section explores the needs of each of the product stakeholders in detail.

Tip Quality software meets all the stakeholders' needs.

1.2.1 Users

A *user* is the person who directly interacts with the software to carry out some task. Users employ the software to increase their productivity, convenience, or pleasure.

Even if a software system provides the right functionality and has an intuitive interface, the user still might refuse to use it if the system inhibits productivity. Users often rely on software as a tool to carry out their jobs. Examples include engineers and draftsmen who use computer-assisted design software, data-entry workers who enter data into databases, travel agents, software developers, bank tellers, writers and editors, and air traffic controllers. These workers and others spend their days in front of terminals interacting with software. Nothing annoys them (and their managers) more than software that interferes with their productivity. It creates an ongoing drain to the business and, in some cases, can put a critical business function at risk.

In practice, the user requirements include:

- **Functionality**—what the software does. Having the right functionality is critical to meeting user needs. For example, software that requires that the same data be entered more than once by the user is lower in quality than software that requires only a single entry. A good example of software with well-thought-out functionality is personal financial software that lets the user pay bills online with a single entry that also updates the check register.

- **Robustness**—ability of the software to perform in unexpected situations. This is a variant of functionality. No matter how good your understanding of requirements, there are likely to be users that find some reasonable, but unexpected way to use your software. Good engineers try to anticipate this situation by designing beyond expected use and providing for more performance than expected. For example, suppose your research shows that no one will ever have more than one instance of your software running at one time. Even so, a robust design should allow for more than one instance, just in case. The art is finding the correct tradeoff between cost of development and deployment and the robust solution. The Y2K crisis is a great example. Unlike its usual characterization as a "bug," the original choice to use two characters for the year was a design choice, but not a robust one. When the software was originally designed, there was a great premium placed on saving memory and storage. The designers did not plan for the software to be in use up to forty years beyond original deployment.

- **Performance**—how fast the software responds to input. Imagine that your word processor takes half a second to put each typed letter on the screen. You would not put up with such software for long. Sometimes performance refers to the time the software takes for a larger background task, like printing a page. If a system takes an hour to print a page of text, it would be less than useful. Another example: users of CAD/CAM systems expect the system to respond to their interactions with a complicated design in less than 0.5 second. If it takes more than 30 seconds for a bank account system to confirm a teller transaction, the teller is less productive and customers become annoyed.

- **Ease of use**—how much effort it takes the user to access the functionality. If it takes too many *gestures*, mouse clicks, or keystrokes to access some important function, the users will find their productivity impaired and dislike the software.

- **Reliability**—a measure of whether the user can rely on the software to consistently respond appropriately to input, not to crash, hang, or to corrupt the user's data. In some cases, reliability can be a matter of safety. I have personal experience with this aspect of reliability. My late-model automobile decided to stall while going full legal speed on a freeway, an annoying and dangerous behavior. It turned out that the repair consisted of a software update to the engine controller. Reliability affects safety in all software used to control automobiles, aircraft, or spacecraft.

Example of User Productivity Support

The air traffic control system is a dramatic example of a system that must support user productivity. The software displays the processes and the radar and transponder data that enable air traffic controllers to assign routes, altitudes, and air speeds. The U.S. Federal Aviation Administration has contracted with Lockheed Corporation for a set of major technological upgrades to the nation's air traffic control system. One of the new systems is called the Display System Replacement (DSR); it displays the situation in the air to the air traffic controllers. The $1 billion system provides the primary interface that the controllers rely on to do their job. In March 1999, Kenneth Mead, Inspector General of the U.S. Department of Transportation, described the DSR to Congress. [Congressional testimony, March 25, 1999, available at http://www.faa.gov/newsroom.htm]

"DSR modernizes en route traffic control centers by replacing aging and unsupportable display equipment. DSR features new color displays and consoles for controllers. It uses modern computer processing technology for improved speed, capacity, maintainability, and reliability. DSR can be upgraded easily with hardware and software enhancements."

In 1997, members of the National Air Traffic Controllers Association (NATCA) were asked, as representatives of the DSR user community, to evaluate the DSR version. Presumably, the developer thought the system met requirements and was ready for deployment. The NATCA members were so alarmed at what they saw, they issued the following policy statement [http://home.natca.org/natca/]:

NATCA Policy: Display System Replacement

Whereas representatives from all ARTCCs scheduled to receive DSR equipment, a representative from San Juan CERAP (ZSU), and the NATCA DSR site and regional representatives assembled in Washington, D.C., on August 12, 1997, for the sole purpose of evaluating the current state of affairs of DSR, and;

Whereas the assembly fully understands that the deteriorating infrastructure of this nation's air traffic control system demands that the enroute display equipment be replaced and/or upgraded as expeditiously as possible, and;

Whereas the collective body, after receiving a full and complete briefing and analysis of the status of DSR, has unanimously determined that the current state of DSR is "operationally unacceptable," and;

Whereas an operationally unacceptable system will:

- Reduce system capacity and efficiency, resulting in higher operating costs to the users of the system;
- Degrade the system's margin of safety; and;
- Increase complexity of air traffic controllers' job function, resulting in a greater risk of error and loss of productivity.

Therefore be it resolved that NATCA shall expeditiously utilize any and all means at its disposal to:

- Demand that the Federal Aviation Administration immediately cease and desist deployment and/or implementation of DSR in its current state, and;
- Compel the FAA to provide a display system replacement which:
  - Is operationally acceptable to the air traffic controllers using the system;
  - Allows controllers to efficiently handle existing and projected increases in traffic volume with the same or higher level of effectiveness as the current system;

- Has no observable system degradation or safety compromise due to difficulties with data entry, displayed data, or for any other reason, and;
- Does not degrade controller health and/or welfare and complies with the Americans with Disabilities Act.

The DSR has now delivered all 20 domestic enroute centers. The first site, Seattle, was dedicated in January 1999, years later than originally planned and greatly over the original budget. The NATCA issues were addressed, and the air traffic controllers are said to be satisfied with the system. In the end, an operational system was delivered.

It seems obvious that DSR system development would have benefited from early and ongoing NATCA involvement to identify and address operational issues throughout the development, not just at the end.

The line between usable and unusable software is very thin, and users are unforgiving. Too often, I have seen system developers sitting in their windowless cubicles expounding on how users *should* use the system. They take strong positions and argue passionately. The problem is that, unless they are a member of the user community or have input from the user community, they have no basis for their opinions. No wonder modern software processes provide for ongoing user involvement, which we will discuss further in Chapter 5.

It is generally impossible to create a usable software product without user participation in the development.

1.2.2 Customers

A *customer* purchases the software. We are all used to thinking about external customers. There also can be internal customers, other organizations in your own company. For example, a product group in a company may contract another team in the same company to provide some embedded software.

Often, software customers are not the users. A corporate information technology department may purchase software on behalf of another department, say, human resources. In another example, the purchaser may embed the purchased software in his or her own product to sell to a third party. Even so, customers are concerned that the users' needs are met. In fact, if your software is being used in the customer's product, they may assume liability for the reliability of your software. If I had an accident due to my automobile stalling, I might have sued the automobile manufacturer, not whoever wrote the engine controller software.

In addition to having a stake in user needs, customers have concerns related to the associated costs of owning and deploying the software. The actual costs of deploying software extend beyond the initial license and maintenance fees. These other costs include installation and customization along with the ongoing mainte-nance tasks such as reporting software defects to the provider, installing patches and updates, and looking after user accounts.

Customers are concerned with organization, not just individual productivity. This concern can result in an increased set of functional requirements, such as the need to be able to install patches while the software is running.

In many instances, the customer organization does not include any users. In these cases, the customer may attempt to represent the needs of the users by gath-ering their requirements and then presenting them in the purchasing contract. To make matters worse, some customers will jealously prevent the software organiza-tion from having any contact with the user. This situation can place an extra bur-den on the software development organization. Its effectiveness in meeting the user needs can be limited by the customer's ability to gather, specify, and manage user requirements. Often one of the software development leader's greatest chal-lenges is developing a constructive, collaborative relationship with the customer in coming to agreement on the user needs. You should do all you can to work with the customers to include user representatives in the development process. This is discussed further in Chapter 5.

In summary, in addition to the user needs, customers are concerned with the following factors.

- **Costs**—Costs of ownership consist of more than the initial purchase costs. Other ownership costs include yearly license maintenance fees, installation costs, cost of organization customization, internal user support, defect reporting, installing patches and updates, training, database maintenance, and additional hardware to host the program. For many software systems, particularly if they are poorly designed, the ownership costs can greatly exceed the initial development costs.

- **Supportability**—Ease of maintenance in the field, usually the efficiency of installing patches and upgrades, contributes to supportability. For example, some software requires the system to be brought down for a week to install a new version. Such software adds greatly to the burden of the purchasing organization and provides an inconvenience to the user.

- **Availability**—The percentage of work time that the system is actually online and available to the user is its availability. It is determined by both the system's reliability and the *mean time to repair* (MTTR), the amount of time it takes to bring a system back up after a failure.

- **Configurability**—The ability to tailor the software to perform well in the customer setting is what is meant by configurability. To perform well under varying loads, software needs varying amount of hardware resources. Customers may not want to adapt their hardware infrastructure to your application; rather they would prefer to configure the software so that it works well in their environment.

1.2.3 Investors

The *investors* are the people or organization that pay for the development. The management of your company or an external firm that contracts the software for their own purposes can be investors. No matter who they are, investors expect a return on their investment. Sometimes they literally expect a profit from the sale of the software or a product containing the software. Sometimes they expect the return in greater productivity of their organization.

Usually the service costs are borne by the investors. Service costs include staffing helplines and creating and distributing product patches. Looking after these costs entails some more attention to the quality of software. These are discussed in the next section.

There is an additional kind of return on investment; the development may result in some *intellectual property*. In the printer example, the investors hoped that the product design would be the basis for an ongoing product line. Similarly, the investors in software development hope that the software design will then be the basis for maintaining market competitiveness. If the software is contracted for customer use, the software code may be reused in some way for lowering the expense for the next contracted system. In some cases, the intellectual property might be sold. The elements of software intellectual property will be discussed further in Chapter 2.

In the end, the investors have three major concerns.

1. The acceptability of the software by the users and customers. The usefulness of the software can create the demand that in turn generates the revenue stream.

2. The service costs, which add expenses that can erode profits.

3. The value of the intellectual property.

The concerns of the users and customers were discussed above; the other issues are discussed below.

Service Costs   As the leader of a development organization, you will probably be focused on development costs. However, if the software is going to have any long-term use, the service costs can often dwarf the development costs. *Service costs* include expenses of manning the technical support phone lines, tracking the problem reports from the field, finding and removing the defects, and building and shipping the patches. For a commercial product, these costs often make the difference between profit and loss. Ironically, the service costs increase with the number of customers. So creating attractive but flawed software can be deadly. For contracted software, the service costs often dwarf the development costs. It follows that building a product that limits the service costs is usually more important than limiting the development expense.

A chief factor that affects the service costs is the software's reliability. If the software often fails under normal use, then you can expect many service calls and a large expense associated with distributing fixes. There is also the associated cost of losing hard-won, but now unsatisfied, customers. The other elements of service costs include supportability, the cost of fixes in the field, and maintainability, the costs of isolating and removing a defect in the code.

Intellectual Property   The intellectual property associated with software, the code base and the design, should have value beyond the initial release. The intellectual property should be the basis for a set of products or an ongoing product line or both. As in the printer example, future products may have unknown requirements.

The value of the intellectual property is seen as a competitive advantage for an investor who is interested in staying ahead of the market. If the software was developed for internal use, the value of the intellectual property comes from the ability of the company to keep up with user needs by adding new features at a reasonable expense.

In the end, both situations come to the same need: The software should be *robust* in that it can be applied to a broadening set of requirements efficiently. The point to remember is that the intellectual value of the software should outlast the initial requirements. This means the value is in the design. Robustness is discussed in more detail in a later section of this chapter.

In the last decade or so, the need to capitalize on the intellectual property of software has resulted in a variety of reuse initiatives. Many reason that if the intellectual value is to be captured, then the software must be reused in whole or in part. The reasoning has led to various schemes to retain and document the parts of the software for reuse. For reasons that will be described in Chapter 2 on software architecture, reuse is a subtle, complicated business, and so most reuse efforts fail.

1.3 QUALITY ATTRIBUTES

The previous section examined quality from the point of view of the stakeholders. This section provides a unified list, with further explanation, of the different dimensions of software quality. You will note that I grouped the attributes of software quality into the broader categories of usability, robustness, and reliability. I believe this framework will help you understand what constitutes quality software.

1.3.1 Usability

One of the most daunting challenges facing most software organizations, as well as some hardware organizations, is to understand how the customer plans to use the product. The printer example illustrates that a small misunderstanding of user needs can lead to serious problems in the field.

Software is often provided to support some complex, mission-critical task. The interactions between the users and the system in carrying out the task must be well understood. Engineers sitting in their cubicles or in design meetings talking among themselves are unlikely to get the design right; they need to interact with the users.

There are two main considerations in building a usable program: The program must have the right functionality and provide an intuitive interface.

Functionality With the right *functionality*, the program does all the things it needs to do. Determining the right functionality can be a challenge. Customers are often imprecise in describing their needs or may not be fully aware of their requirements for the system. It takes effort to help customers understand and specify what they want. All too often, the true requirements do not become evident until a system is fielded.

Consider an assignment to build a record system for student grades. Requirements are given: "Maintain records of student grades. Compute final grades and print a report that shows individual grades and class distribution. Print report cards automatically, and archive the grades. Provide a summary report to the principal's office."

This sounds like a simple database application. The developer creates three entry screens: one for entering students' names and their grades, one for listing the class exams, and one for the exam and assignment weightings to be used in calculating the final grade. This seems to be an efficient design because the exams and the weightings can be entered for the whole class at once rather than individually.

However, when the staff tries to use the application, they find that the requirements and the design are inadequate. For example, the system does not allow tests to count on an individual basis. This means that the program gives incorrect data for students who enrolled late or who were excused from an exam. The program accepts numeric grades but not pass/fail ratings. It cannot deal with situations in which students quit the class early because of illness or relocation. Will they be reported as having failed? The teachers soon realize that the program is inadequate. They abandon the system and revert to keeping handwritten grade books.

The difficulty of providing the right functionality is not only a problem for user applications; it is also a challenge for developers of embedded software. If the engineer of some system with embedded software specifies that the software-driven subsystem do something that was not anticipated by the designers, it is likely to cause a freeze ("hang up"), or worse. When users experience this behavior, they think you built a flawed system.

Intuitive Interface With an *intuitive interface*, the system behaves as the user expects. Any time you rent a car, regardless of the make and model, you are ready to drive within a few minutes. You can quickly determine how to drive the car once you have figured out how to turn on the headlights. The rest is standard: The accelerator is always to the right of the brake, the turn signal is always a lever on the steering wheel shaft, and so on. Experiments with the human-car interface, such as digital speedometers, are approached carefully and usually fail. This standardization of the interface has promoted efficiency in the industry and among users. Car manufacturers can be confident that usability concerns will not have an impact on sales. The interface is intuitive and customers can confidently drive any vehicle with minimal or no training.

Nothing is more annoying to a user than to be faced with an unfathomable interface. Software designers are challenged to make all the marvelous functionality of a system available to the user in a way that seems natural and as standard as possible. No matter how much functionality your program provides, it is useless if the user cannot access it. Not long ago, programs for personal computers made their functionality available through typed commands and function keys (those keys labeled F1 through F12 at the top of the keyboard). The interface required the user to memorize the key associated with each command—not through an intuitive understanding of the command.

Today, graphical user interfaces with icons remind us of the function they provide. Both the Windows and the Mac environments have standard rules for interfacing with a program. In Windows, the file menu is always on the far left side of the menu bar and always contains the "open" and "save" commands. This is a great help, but it does not fully solve the problem of providing an intuitive interface.

The interface of unique application functions should always be as natural as possible. For example, Microsoft Project is a powerful and useful tool that is plagued with interface issues. Its users are always struggling to figure out or remember how to access some function. Most neophytes give up and use spreadsheets.

Developing an intuitive interface requires an understanding of users and how they do their work. The same function may have a different interface in a different program. For example, both Adobe Illustrator, which targets commercial artists, and AutoCAD, which targets engineers and draftsmen, provide the user with a way of drawing lines. However, the interfaces are very different. Your team must be sophisticated enough to understand such subtleties. They need some mechanism for reviewing the interface with the targeted user.

1.3.2 Robustness

All products, including software, are designed to operate under a certain set of conditions. Sometimes these conditions are explicit, sometimes implicit. For example, the printer design team assumed that the users would be interested primarily in printing text files and that the printer's performance for other kinds of documents did not matter. They may never explicitly have expressed this decision, but just implicitly assumed it when developing their design and tests. They may have been relying on market research data that was wrong or out of date. In any case, this turned out to be a bad assumption.

A *robust* product is designed to operate well beyond the set of design assumptions. For example, it is reasonable to expect that an automobile will never be operated above 90 mph. However, it is essential that the automobile function at some higher speed, say, 120 mph. Otherwise, problems may arise on very rare occasions. For a fielded product such as an automobile, rare occasions can turn into hundreds or thousand of incidents. These in turn can lead to high service or liability costs or at the least a market perception of poor quality. So whereas a given level of robustness adds cost to the product, it can also add an essential margin of safety and reliability.

Not only did the printer design team make uninformed assumptions about customer needs, they produced a design that was not robust. A robust design would have provided for printing graphics as well as text. A printer with this more robust design would have been found more acceptable by the users. Because robustness comes at a cost, leading the team to an appropriate tradeoff is one of the challenges of development management.

Just like the printer design team, software designers must make assumptions about the use and applicability of a program. Examples include the number of simultaneous users of a Web page, and the number of data items that must be stored in a database. The assumptions may be subtler, such as the minimal acceptable system response time for a given task. Designing too tightly to these expectations will lead to an unacceptable product.

As a leader, you have a serious stake in delivering robust software. You need a way to determine whether software under development is robust. Hold conversations on this topic; it is important to have a shared vocabulary. Schedule and attend project reviews. At the meetings, ask questions designed to uncover the assumptions underlying the design. For example, ask the team to describe the user and how the product will be used. Ask about capacity and performance expectations. Ask how these assumptions are reflected in the design. Then ask the clincher: What happens if they are wrong, if the assumption proves to be incorrect? Listen carefully to the answer. If the team says that it will never happen, you are probably in trouble. It is time for a serious design assessment.

There are other indicators that system design may not be robust.

- Hostility toward customers by your engineers

- Discussions with customers during which the engineers maintain that the customers are misusing the software

- A general lack of awareness or current understanding of how the customer will use the product

- Impassioned speeches by your developers on what the customer needs that are not based on objective data

If you notice any of these signs, start asking questions. If necessary, add designers with more experience to your design team.

Capacity   *Capacity* refers to the number of things the software can handle. These things can be the number of simultaneous users, data items, open windows, or the like. Often capacity is tied to performance. Capacity itself has two dimensions. There is absolute capacity—built-in limits—and there is useful capacity—the number of things the software can handle before it becomes too slow to be useful.

Although not as common as it used to be, software can be designed with a fixed capacity. For example, the system may support only ten users at a time; the eleventh receives a message that the application is not available. Alternatively, a user may add a data record only to be told that his database is full and items must be removed before another record can be stored. This is a cell-phone-type design with a fixed number of slots for phone numbers. These hardwired limits can be an indication of bad design.

What is more common is for the software to have no limit to the number of users or data items, but simply to slow down with increased capacity. Note that in your Palm Pilot there is no limit in the software as to the number of contacts or memos you can store. The software will allocate the existing memory to accommodate items as needed. If you run out of space, you can add more memory. All that happens as you add items is that the searches take longer. It follows that useful capacity is really tied to performance.

Scalability   *Scalability* is the ability of the software to handle increasing capacity (see the previous discussion on Capacity). Robust software is scalable since it can accommodate capacity beyond the initial requirements. Consider this example of a nonscalable program, a database of donors and their contributions for nonprofit organizations. The team assumes that no contributor will make more than 50 donations. They make this assumption with no user input. They fail to allow for the reasonable scenario of a donor who makes monthly donations for more than four years. The team might create a donor data structure with places for 50 donations for each donor. Although this is a simple, high-performance approach, it does not allow the user to add the 51st entry. (A lot of early software for personal computers was written this way.) An alternative would be to create a more sophisticated approach to storing the data; that is, storing the donations and the donors as separate files, with links between them. This approach contains no hardwired limits. There is no fixed number of donations for any donor. As the number of donations increases, the system response time increases. At some large number of entries, system performance could be so slow that the product becomes unusable. In this case, the system would fail gracefully. The system should be defined so that the number of entries leading to unacceptable performance is so high (for example, 10,000 donations) that it is unlikely to be reached. The second design is robust; the first is not.

Extendability Most software systems have more than one release. Some releases have defects removed but have little or no functionality. They are called point (or maintenance) releases because they are usually numbered 1.X, such as WormGrower v1.1. If the system is successful, you will have the opportunity to develop a functional release, which will have new features or enhancements. In our printer example, the ability to support WebPrint would require a functional enhancement. As a manager, you need to anticipate functional enhancements. Your goal should be to deliver enhancements to the field in time to meet market or customer needs. For a product to be profitable or affordable, the cost of adding enhancements should be as low as possible.

Software engineers need to make sure that the software design anticipates business needs, especially enhancements. A design that accommodates enhancements is said to be *extendable*. In practice, extendibility is achieved with the same discipline that leads to a maintainable design: by having a clear, well-thought-out model of the system. If the code is not maintainable, it will not be extendible.

Configurability Of course, the customer may want to limit the number of users in order to ensure a minimum response time for users. In this case the software may have unlimited absolute capacity, but needs to be *configurable* to limit access in order to preserve responsiveness. You often see this limitation in Web applications. The limit can be raised by providing more hardware support. Similarly, the customer may want to limit data space for users, again to preserve a level of quality for all. An example would be an e-mail application that limits the number of items in the mailbox or a voice-mail system that limits the number of stored messages. The point is that the software has no intrinsic limits; it provides quality by having the useful limits determined by the available hardware resources and because it can be configured by the customer.

Portability   Another dimension of configurability is *portability*—the ability to host the software on a variety of hardware platforms. For example, the software may run on a Windows, Intel platform, but if portable, it can be moved to a Linux platform without redesign. Portability provides you and your investors flexibility in approaching the market. Whether to take advantage of the portability and to field versions on a variety of platforms is a market decision based on the costs of additional testing, configuration management, and field support.

Portability often comes at a performance cost. Generally, software loses portability when the designers take advantage of special features of the hardware to achieve performance. To achieve portability, the designers need to forgo using these features and use general mechanisms. It gets worse; the identical code can perform differently on different platforms and so performance is always an issue with portability.

Portability is achieved through careful design. A good design approach is to have a so-called *abstraction layer* that partitions the hardware-specific functionality from the rest of the code. Such software, even though it requires some limited amount of special code per platform, is still considered portable. A well-designed abstraction layer can provide a good compromise between the cost of porting and the platform-specific performance.

If portability is a concern, be sure to review with your team the costs, tradeoffs, and approach to its accomplishment.

1.3.3 Reliability

Defects are best thought of in terms of their probability of occurring. Most users use the software in a similar manner; they put the software through similar execution paths. These paths should be understood and thoroughly tested. The software should be rock solid for these paths. Any defect in the software that arises in these scenarios will occur very often in the field, resulting in very unreliable software. Every so often, a user will find some unexpected way of using the software. Errors that arise in these situations are harder to find and to remove. In fact, finding these execution paths may take hundreds of hours of testing. To find them requires an automated testing capability that simulates different users, or putting the code into many users' hands prior to shipment. This early user testing is reason for beta testing. In practice, for good software, defects are easily discovered and removed in the early testing. Bad software just crashes, making defect discovery and removal difficult. As the testing continues, the reliability improves, and it gets harder and more expensive to find the next defect. Research supports the intuition that the

cost of finding defects grows geometrically. For instance, the cost of finding the fif-
tieth defect might be ten times the cost of finding the third defect. Eventually, the
leader has to decide when enough is enough—that the cost of testing and loss of
market opportunity balance the expected service costs. It is at that point the product is ready to be shipped.

Mean Time between Failures   Software is reliable if the average time
between inappropriate responses—its *mean time between failures* (MTBF)—is
longer than the time the program needs to stay up in order to be usable. Inappropriate responses include crashes, hangs, data corruptions, or anything else that
interferes with the software being used for its intended purpose.

If a program crashes after a couple of minutes, it is probably useless. A word
processor needs to stay up for a working day or so, airline reservation systems for
days at a time. Generally, MTBF is a better measure of software quality than the
number of defects. Defects found in corners of the code so unlikely to be reached
that they do not interfere with the program's normal use are of little consequence.
Measuring MTBF determines how likely it is that the remaining defects will be
encountered. If the MBTF is high enough, the expense of finding the remaining
defects may not be warranted.

Availability   *Availability* is the percentage of time that the software is available for use by the users. At first blush, a system that is 99.9% available might
sound good. However, as Table 1-1 shows, this software will be down 3.65 days in a

Table 1-1 Downtime by Levels of Availability

Availability	Downtime			
	Seconds	**Minutes**	**Hours**	**Days**
99.99999%	3.153599998	0.05256	0.000876	3.65E–05
99.99990%	31.536	0.5256	0.00876	0.000365
99.99900%	315.36	5.256	0.0876	0.00365
99.99000%	3,153.6	52.56	0.876	0.0365
99.90000%	31,536	525.6	8.76	0.365
99.00000%	315,360	5,256	87.6	3.65
90.00000%	3,153,600	52,560	876	36.5

365-day year. Note that software that is 99.999% available is down for 5 minutes a year, a level good enough for a bank or a travel reservation system, but maybe not good enough for a phone system. At this writing, the availability of the air traffic control system appears to be around 99.9%, an unacceptable value.

Usually, to be available the program must have a large MBTF. In addition, availability means the time to error recovery must be managed. It follows that achieving high availability requires a set of specific techniques. For example, it may require redundant hardware or using automated error detection and reload.

Generally, achieving high levels of availability takes significant development time and expense. One of the challenges a leader faces is making the trade between this cost and schedule and delivering adequate availability.

Repairability *Repairability* has two dimensions that are easily confused:

- **Maintainability**—ease of correcting defects in the design
- **Supportability**—ease of servicing the product in the field

Note these terms have restricted technical meanings; common parlance confuses the terms. The second, more common definition is the expense of servicing the product in the field. The 1960 VW Beetles were easy to support; Porsches are not. If a printer were designed so that it had to be brought to a dealer to replace a print cartridge, its field supportability would be unacceptable.

Maintainability Software developers must be concerned with the narrower definition of maintainability. A *defect* is defined as some aspect of the system that interferes with the system meeting its intended purpose. Defects can be caused by errors in design implementation or by a misunderstanding of the requirements. In the latter case, the system is built as designed, but the design was wrong. A system is *maintainable* if it is economically efficient to correct system defects. In the printer story, field experience revealed that soldering the power supply to the printer controller was a design defect. It prevented the printer from being shipped to the customer in a usable condition. The tragedy was not that there was a defect, but that there was no affordable way to correct it. The system was not maintainable.

A defect is not a tragedy. The tragedy occurs when there is no way to correct the defect.

Some software is maintainable; some is not. Software is usually maintainable when the design of the system clearly specifies what each piece of the software does. A well-designed system supports maintainability in two ways:

- Sources of defects are readily identified.

- Removing a defect does not introduce another defect.

One sign of code that is poorly designed is brittleness; every time the code is touched to fix a problem, it breaks somewhere else. Brittle code is usually a disaster. No matter how much effort is expended in the hope that the next fix will do the trick, the code never passes the system test. Often it must be abandoned and redesigned.

Given the complexity of software systems, it is much more reasonable to bet that the system will have defects that need to be addressed than that it will be flawless once it is released. For most systems, the cost of field maintenance far outweighs the cost of initial development, and the cost of ensuring system maintainability will be recouped many times over. The wise, aware manager will strive to anticipate the design maintenance and make it affordable.

Supportability   Recall that software versions come in two flavors: upgrades that provide new functionality and patches that remove defects without affecting functionality. *Supportable* software is easy to upgrade or patch in the field. The most supportable software can be upgraded or patched while running. If every patch or upgrade requires that the software stop and the system be rebooted, then users and customers are faced with making a trade between the cost and inconvenience of loading the patch and the risk of leaving the defect on the system.

Software that is not supportable can have poor availability because of the downtime associated with the upgrades. Many of us have experienced messages from the IT department containing the news that a program will not be available while a new version is being installed. Providing highly supportable software, then, provides value to your customers, but as with other quality attributes, this software requires attention. Often teams, in designing the software, are so concerned with the functional requirements of the software, they neglect to address supportability. As we will discuss in the next chapter, supportability can be captured as a specific kind of requirement for the software.

1.4 WHAT PRICE QUALITY?

Managers may wonder whether they can afford the cost of developing a quality system. After all, it takes effort to ensure a robust, reliable design, and effort costs time and money. How much quality can the project afford?

The answer comes in two parts. First, determine the priority of the quality attributes to your stakeholders. Do all you can to make informed tradeoffs. You should have a good understanding of the needs of the stakeholders, and the right amount of quality for your market. By example, is the cost of achieving 99.9999% availability justified, or is 99.999% good enough for your software? Sometimes reliability for a limited functionality is more important than providing every bell and whistle with less reliability. Telephone switch or manufacturing process control software would make these tradeoffs. Other times, such as in research prototypes, functionality matters more.

Once this understanding is achieved, then providing quality is free. To see why quality more than pays for itself, consider a software product or software embedded in a manufactured product. In this case, the software development is either all or part of the research and development cost of the product development. Fixed R&D costs typically represent 10 to 20% of the cost of fielding the product. However, the service costs grow proportionally with the number of products sold. If you are very unlucky, you can have a very successful, flawed product. The costs of servicing the warranty can easily dwarf R&D costs and erode profits. If you are less unlucky, the flaws will be apparent early enough that you will not sell any products. In either case, even increasing R&D costs by 50% to achieve the needed quality is more than justified in the context of the business case. In the end, the lack of quality is not only more expensive, it is catastrophic.

The situation is not very different whether you are building software to be used by your organization or to serve some business function. In most cases, the cost of the redesign and the loss of productivity within your organization far outweigh any additional development costs.

One of the challenges you as a leader will face is deciding if the software is good enough. This decision is based on whether the cost of not shipping is greater than the service costs for the shipped product. The cost of not shipping may include missing a market window or not delivering on a contract. More experienced managers may ship early enough to capture the market with the intention of putting out a service release soon enough to limit the service costs that are expected, given the known levels of defects. This is a very reasonable approach, but requires the leader not only to have a solid understanding of the market but also to know the true status of the code. How to achieve this understanding is contained in the remainder of the book.

1.5 THE ZERO-DEFECT TRAP

A common erroneous characterization of quality software is that it meets requirements and is virtually defect-free. Zero-defect programs are effective for refining processes used to carry out any repeated task, such as manufacturing a light bulb or delivering a letter. They cannot be applied successfully to software development; code is not manufactured like light bulbs: Each line of code is unique and is best thought of as an element in the detailed design.

Any organization that tries to apply a standard based on defects per line of code will be very frustrated because defects become increasingly difficult and expensive to find. As one defect is found and removed, the amount of testing time it takes to find the next defect increases dramatically. Eventually, finding the next defect becomes unaffordable. If finding the next defect would take 40 hours of testing by 20 programmers, you might decide to go ahead and ship. It is generally impossible to find the last defect, that is, to ship a defect-free system. To attain that standard would take more testing than any organization could afford.

Testing is limited as a means to ensure quality. In her text *Safeware*, Nancy Leveson [Leveson, 1995] gives examples of safety-critical, mature software systems that after extensive testing and thousands of hours of use were still found to have residual errors. She goes on to state, "[R]eliability assessment by testing at the system level is impractical in any complex system."

Even though defect discovery and removal is essential, the number of defects in the code is not the only important view of software quality. Systems are often unacceptable because of a design defect. The code may work as the programmers intended, passing all the tests, and still be unusable because the developers did not really understand what the users needed.

1.6 THE BOTTOM LINE: QUALITY BY DESIGN

Like in the printer example, the real pain of a project often starts once the code is shipped. As in the printer example, you can ship a product that meets all the stated requirements, passes all the tests, on time and on budget, and still fail to meet the real need needs of the stakeholders. Success requires that you ship usable, robust, maintainable, reliable, extendable software. Achieving these ends is a matter of design.

Here are four things you need to do to make sure that your organization delivers quality products:

1. Arrange for the ongoing involvement of the user representatives throughout the development.

2. Invest in the creation and maintenance of system architecture, discussed in Chapter 2, and insist that the code follow the architecture.

3. Determine your quality priorities and communicate the priorities to your team.

4. Ask your team how the different dimensions are addressed in the architecture and be sure you understand and are comfortable with the answers.

To Learn More

This readable text explains usability issues in detail:

- Raskin, Jef. *The Humane Interface: New Directions for Designing Interactive Systems,* Addison-Wesley, 2000.

This text addresses several quality issues with insight and experience. It provides useful guidance on the limitations and role of testing:

- Leveson, Nancy G. *Safeware: System Safety and Computers,* Addison-Wesley, 1995.

The following are good references on manufacturing quality:

- Harry, Mikel and Richard Schroeder. *Six Sigma, the Breakthrough Management Strategy Revolutionizing the World's Top Corporations,* Doubleday, 1999.

- Clausing, Donald. *Total Quality Development: A Step-By-Step Guide to World Class Concurrent Engineering,* American Society of Mechanical Engineers, 1994.

Chapter 2

Software Architecture

Software quality is a matter of design. This chapter introduces the standard diagrams for specifying software design. The chapter concludes with a discussion of how the diagrams are used to address the quality issues raised in Chapter 1, along with suggestions on the role the leader should play in facilitating quality.

Chapter 1 described quality software; this chapter begins the discussion about how quality is achieved. One of the lessons of Chapter 1 is that achieving quality is more than meeting requirements and being defect free; it is meeting the needs of the users, customers, and investors. To meet those needs, the software must be sufficiently well designed.

Software design, often called the *software architecture*, serves three important needs:

- It provides the views to address the need for quality software, as discussed in Chapter 1.

- It constitutes the intellectual property that provides your organization a competitive advantage.

- It enables your team to efficiently develop software by providing a common, consistent specification of the system.

The remainder of this chapter introduces the elements of software architecture and of various views that address the various quality concerns. The chapter goes on to discuss how tools can help automate development of software architecture. The chapter concludes with a review of how software architecture can facilitate the creation of quality software. The use of architecture in the development process is also described in some detail in Chapter 3.

2.1 ARCHITECTURE DEFINED

James Rumbaugh, a leading expert in software design, defines architecture as "the organizational structure of a system, including its decomposition into parts, their connectivity, interaction mechanisms, and the guiding principles that inform the design of the system" [Rumbaugh, 1999]. A system needs to be described in terms of parts, with each part responsible for a well-defined set of services. The parts collaborate in understandable ways to carry out the functionality required of the system. All interfaces between the parts need to be documented. The *software architecture* is expressed by a set of diagrams that captures the parts and how they work together.

As a manager, you must understand the architecture of your system. A good approach is to think of the software as a system of subsystems. A modern automobile provides a useful analogy. It consists of well-understood subsystems: the drive train, suspension, electrical, exhaust, HVAC (heating, ventilation, and air conditioning), braking, instrumentation, body and chassis, and network subsystems. Each subsystem has clear responsibilities in meeting the functional requirements of the automobile.

To an engineer, the automobile is a coupled assemblage of these subsystems. There are many requirements for coupling: The under-hood area must accommodate the engine; the engine must provide power to the air conditioner and heat to the heating coils; the electrical system must provide power to start the engine; the engine must provide power to recharge the battery.

Different companies may produce the various subsystems. Sometimes the manufacturer changes a subsystem based on the economics of working with the supplier. Sometimes the manufacturer gives the buyer options, such as standard or heavy-duty brakes. Modularity of design for a system as complex as an automobile has led to a very efficient industry. Because of the modularity of design, design defects are easily addressed. Recalls occur, but they tend to have minimal impact on the overall design.

Each subsystem has its own architecture. For example, the drive train consists of the engine, transmission, drive shaft, and differential. The subsystems are usually more cohesive in their design than the overall system. It would be unwise to replace the engine with a larger one without checking whether the transmission could handle the increased torque. The design of drive train components is even more tightly coupled.

Like the automobile, well-designed software has easily identified subsystems with well-defined responsibilities. The subsystems are loosely coupled in that they interact minimally and to some extent independently. Some common examples of software subsystems are business rule parsers used in workflow automation software, event handlers used in some simulation systems, persistence data handlers used to store and retrieve data, and protocol handlers for streaming data across networks. The Unified Modeling Language (discussed later) provides diagrams that express the system modularity. The manager and the team use these diagrams to achieve a common view of the system.

Just as you can comprehend the architecture of an automobile even though you are not an automotive engineer, you should be able to understand the architecture of your organization's software. You may not be able to design a differential, but you understand what a differential does and its importance in the overall system. You can ask intelligent questions about the choice of a differential in the system and understand the answers. This is also true for software. You should insist that the design of any system under your management be sufficiently well architected so that you can understand it. The subsystems, their responsibilities, and how they interact should be clear.

2.2 SPECIFYING SOFTWARE ARCHITECTURE

Until about five years ago, a variety of options existed for specifying software architecture. Although most of these have fallen into disuse, today there remain three kinds of choices:

- The Unified Modeling Language (UML), which is the industry standard for software specification

- Architectural frameworks from other fields such as system engineering

- Ad hoc specifications made up by members of your organization

Of these choices, for reasons explained below, the UML is far superior.

The Unified Modeling Language   *The Unified Modeling Language* (UML) is a standard maintained by the Object Management Group (OMG), a not-for-profit corporation. OMG was founded by 11 companies "to create a component-based software marketplace by hastening the introduction of standardized object software" [Object Management Group, 2000]. It is fair to say that Rational Software contributed most to the specification of UML. The other companies that contributed to the initial specification of UML include Unisys, Hewlett-Packard, Taskon, IBM, Reich, i-Logix, Softeam, ICON Computing, Intellicorp, MCI Systemhouse, Microsoft, ObjecTime, Oracle, Ptech, Platinum, and Sterling Software. UML is continually being revised and enhanced. The Object Management Group (OMG) Web site, www.omg.org, provides the latest status of UML.

As an industry standard, UML has significant advantages over other approaches:

- The diagrams are unambiguous and well documented, characteristics that foster communication.

- Employees new to the project or the company are likely to be familiar with UML, making them productive more quickly.

- The intellectual property of the system architecture will be preserved because others can understand the project architecture after the development is complete.

UML is applied best in object-oriented development. Although objects may have been controversial at one time, that discussion is over: Object-based development is the method of choice for accomplishing quality software development. All progress in tools and methodologies centers on this approach. (Do not be distracted by the recent literature on component-based development; it is a variant of object-based development.)

Other Architectural Frameworks   Sometimes the software is a part of a larger effort such as system design, enterprise re-engineering, embedded devices, product design, or some very special system such as a military command and control or an intelligence system. Practitioners in these domains often have adopted specific frameworks for specifying the architecture. Some examples include IDEF for systems, and the Zachman framework for enterprise modeling.

Sometimes the customers have their own frameworks. For them, the benefits of using the framework are similar to those of adopting the UML: improved team communication, higher productivity, and return on investment. An extensive example is the United States Department of Defense Joint Technical Architecture found on www-jta.itsi.disa.mil.

Idiosyncratic Specification   Imagine that you have hired an architect to design a building. He delivers the design, not as a standard set of blueprints, but in a notation no one has ever seen before: arrows, loops, and boxes. He explains that his diagrams improve on traditional methods of capturing design and points out that they capture on each figure not only the layout of the building but also the way in which the traffic is expected to flow.

You are not impressed. You cannot see how the electricians and plumbers will be able to implement the design, and you are sure the diagrams will not be sufficient to obtain a building permit. No matter how brilliant the design may be, you will probably find the architect's efforts to be unacceptable. You will not be persuaded by his argument that following the standard notation would have interfered with the design process.

You should insist that your organization follow the industry standard when designing software. If every architect and designer were allowed to use whatever notation they liked for blueprints, the result would be misunderstandings, expensive reworkings, and failed products. The same is true for software.

Many software developers will throw an "architecture diagram" on the wall that is not one of the standard views. Everyone in the room may interpret it differently. I have attended far too many meetings where architecture was presented and discussed, with everyone nodding in agreement, only to discover from later conversations that no two people in the room had the same understanding of the diagram. This phenomenon indicates the immaturity of the industry.

Software managers should not be willing to accept nonstandard software design specifications without question.

The Best Choice   If possible, your organization should adopt the UML for specifying the software architecture. If your organization does not have UML-based design and object-based development as a core competency, you will not remain competitive.

Sometimes customers or investors insist that some other framework be adopted. If the customer insists on another framework, then of course you have to accommodate. Even so, you should use UML as much as possible. This challenge is often made easier by the fact that many other frameworks share views with UML. For example, system engineers often use activity and state diagrams, and the same diagrams are found in UML. In addition, there is an ongoing effort to extend UML into software-related domains such as business modeling, data modeling, and system engineering. You may be able to work with your customer to jointly accept UML along with the extensions. See the references at the end of the chapter for more ideas on this topic.

In all instances, avoid any idiosyncratic diagrams. You should be alarmed if you find your team indulging in these diagrams; you should take remedial action. Examples of remediation include assessing UML skills and providing training or a pointed discussion of the needs and benefits of adhering to the standard.

2.3 SOFTWARE ARCHITECTURE

Using UML, your team creates a set of views of the architecture. The different views address different concerns. Here are some of the most common views.

- The *use case* view, which addresses the functionality and behavior of the system

- The *logical* view, which addresses system structure

- The *component* view, which addresses how the logical elements are packaged into the delivered system

- The *deployment* view, which maps the software components to the hosting hardware

Each of these views contains one or more UML diagrams, which capture the design decisions about how the view's concerns are addressed. In addition there are collaboration diagrams which show how the elements in the views work together to meet the software requirements. The views and the associated diagrams are described below.

These views provide different perspectives of the same software architecture model. They enable the different stakeholders and team members to address different quality issues while maintaining design consistency. Although, as a manager, you need not fully understand UML, you should be aware of the views of the system and the purposes they serve.

The different views enable the different stakeholders and team members to work with the system to determine whether it will perform as planned. Each view provides a setting for addressing different quality issues.

2.3.1 Use Case View

Traditional requirements specifications consist of long lists or databases of "shall" statements, such as "the system *shall* maintain at least 10,000 student records." Experience has shown that while these *shall* statements are useful for some requirements, they do not express how the system needs to behave to gain user acceptance. A system could satisfy all the *shalls* and still fail in the field.

There is a more effective way to capture software requirements than *shalls*, a way that focuses on how the users will interact with the system: use cases. Each *use case* describes a set of interactions between the system and the outside world. In UML, use cases are the entities that are captured in use case diagrams. Figure 2-1 shows an example. In the diagram, the external entities, such as system users and other systems, are called actors. Actors are expressed as stick figures, and use cases are represented by ovals. A line between an actor and a use case means that the use case is used by the actor. The set of use cases consists of the things the system must

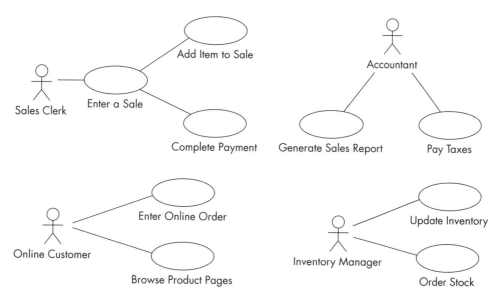

Figure 2-1 Use Case Diagram Example

do to meet the needs of the actors as they use the system to fulfill some business need. Relationships between use cases are expressed as lines.

Use case specifications consist mainly of one or more scenarios (see Figure 2-2). A scenario is a text narrative that describes the steps of the interaction between the actor and the system. The description of the interaction is done without any reference to the internal pieces of the system. The rows in the scenario make up a detailed narrative, in simple English, that describes how the actor and the system interact to carry out the use case. Much of the value of the use cases is found in these descriptions. Use case scenarios describe not only the common or standard operation (sometimes called the blue-sky scenario), but also alternate flows associated with error conditions, system failures, and so on. (See the last entry in the system column in Figure 2-2.) Consequently, there can be more than one scenario per use case.

For example, if you are building a system for retail sales, the actors might include the sales clerk (a person), the credit card validation system (an external system), the accountant, and the inventory manager. The use cases are determined

Step	Actor	System	Constraint
1	This use case begins when the clerk pushes the New Sale button.	The system brings up New Sale screen and the Customer screen for clerk A and enables the scanner.	Total response time is one second.
2	The clerk scans the items and enters the quantity on the keyboard.	The system displays the name and price for each item scanned.	Total response time is one second.
3	The clerk pushes the Total button.	The system computes and displays the total price of the items and the sales taxes.	
4	The clerk swipes the credit card.	If the credit card is valid, the system prints out a receipt, updates the inventory, sends the transaction to the accounting department, and clears the terminal. This ends the use case. If the credit card is not valid, the system sends a Rejected message to the terminal. This ends the use case.	

Figure 2-2 Example Use Case Scenario

based on the set of interactions between the system and the actors that are needed to carry out the activities in the business model.

Examples of use cases for a retail sales system could include checking out a customer, beginning a sale, adding an item to a sale, completing a sale, and validating a credit card. In each use case, the actor (in this case a salesclerk) conducts a series of interactions with the system to support the business need of checking out the customer. Each use case describes a function that must be provided by the system. The list of use cases that must be satisfied by the system is called the *use case survey.*

There is a relationship between the various use cases and the actors, and between the use cases: To *Check Out a Customer,* the Sales Clerk must *Begin a Sale,* repeatedly *Add an Item to a Sale,* and *Complete a Sale.* Figure 2-1 is a use case model for a retail sales system. It shows that the use case supports online customers as actors who can use the system to make online sales.

Use cases are particularly effective because they facilitate communications between the users and the developers. By reading the use case specifications, the users can understand what to expect from the system. The use case scenarios also provide a great head start in creating the system test cases.

For example, suppose the development team reviews the use case model with a set of users. During the review, a clerk asks how to deal with manufacturers' coupons. The development team realizes that a use case is missing and updates the model as shown in Figure 2-3.

Some system requirements cannot be captured as use cases. Examples include system availability (percentage of time the system is up and running) and data capacity. These are called supplemental requirements. The use cases and the supplemental requirements make up the total set of system requirements.

The use case view is used to address the adequacy of the system in meeting the needs of all users.

2.3.2 Logical View

In object-oriented programming, the smallest software part is an object. Each kind of object in the system is described by its *class specification*, which consists of *class attributes*. These are the variables that describe the state of objects of that class. In addition, *methods* are described that other objects can use to access the functionality. For example in our retail sales system, there is an object class called "sales list." The attributes of a sales list are the number of items in the list, a linked list of references to items in the list, the *taxable total,* the *current total,* and the sales

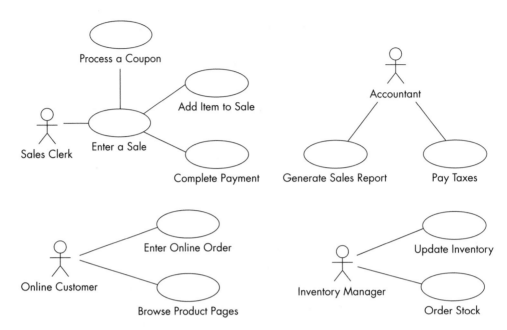

Figure 2-3 Updated Use Case Diagram with Coupon Processing

tax. The methods are *new,* which creates the sales list object, *add_item,* which adds an item to the list, *get_taxable_total, get_tax,* and *get_total,* each of which returns the current value.

Class diagrams exhibit the classes, their specifications, and how objects specified by the various classes interact. Figure 2-4 shows an example of a UML class diagram. Each box represents a class. The class symbol has three horizontal blocks. The top block contains the name of the class. The second block lists the class attributes; the third block lists the operations. The relationships between class objects are shown by the lines between them. For example, Figure 2-4 shows two classes: Sales List and Sales Item. The line with the little diamond denotes that a Sales List contains a list of Sales Items.

Object-based design is effective because objects denote independent blocks of executing code that have well-documented interactions. In our example, the development team updated the model to include coupon processing simply by adding one more class and adding some functionality to the sales list class, as shown in Figure 2-5. The ease of updating the model is an example of the power of the approach: The change was small and well contained.

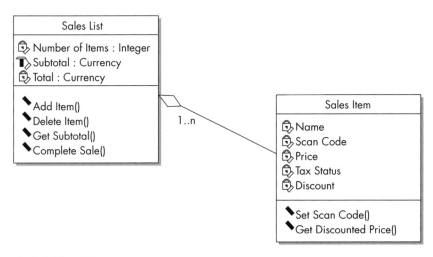

Figure 2-4 A Class Diagram

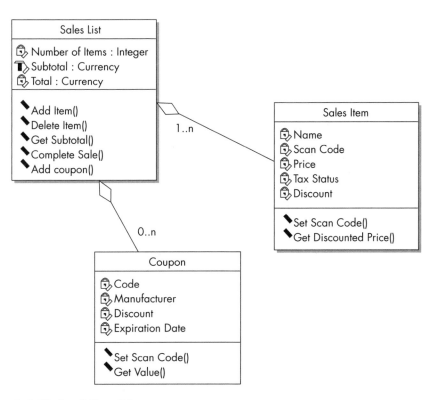

Figure 2-5 Updated Class Diagram

Classes whose objects work together to provide a service to the system are often collected into a class package. Figure 2-6 is a UML diagram that shows the packages that make up the subsystem architecture of the example retail store system. In the diagram, the folders represent the class packages, and the arrows signify how the packages work together. An arrow from one package to another package means that the first package relies on the services of the second package to carry out its activities. The first package depends on the second one. In this situation, the second package has no dependency, so it can be developed independently of the first. Figure 2-6 shows the classes in the order processing package.

Let's return to the automobile analogy. In this case the packages might specify a differential or a muffler. In a well-architected system, the role of the packages should be easily understood by an intelligent, interested manager. Packages that work together can also be grouped. In UML, these groups of packages are still called packages.

Because each class package plays an understandable role, as listed in Figure 2-7, and has an understandable interaction, the subsystems provide a good basis for partitioning the effort. Different developers can work on different subsystems and not get in each other's way.

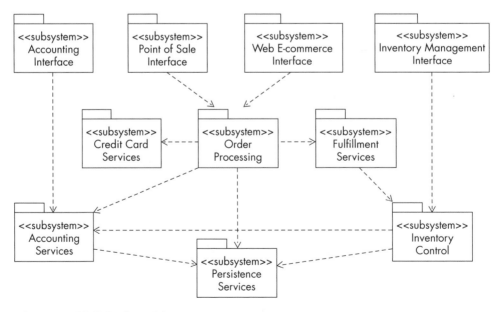

Figure 2-6 UML Package Diagram

Subsystem	Responsibility
Accounting interface	Access screens for accountants
Point-of-sale interface	Enables sales entries
Web e-commerce interface	Provide Web pages for online access
Inventory management interface	Access screens for inventory management
Order processing	Manage in-process orders
Credit card services	Interface with credit card systems, providing validation services
Fulfillment services	Handle interactions with warehouse and shipping services
Accounting services	Maintain accounts
Inventory control	Track inventory
Persistence services	General database services used by other services

Figure 2-7 Subsystem Responsibilities

It is useful to define a subsystem as one of the packages in the top-level architecture of the system. The subsystems are the largest parts of the system in the logical view. Internally, the subsystem may have packages (sub-subsystems) or classes. (Remember that packages can contain packages.) The manager should be able to understand the decomposition of the system, that is, the top-level architecture (low-level detail), just as you can understand the high-level design of a car. Your team should be able to explain the purpose of each subsystem and the reasons for the dependencies. If they cannot, there is probably a design problem.

One subtle aspect of object-oriented design is the relationship between use cases and subsystems. Newcomers to object design often believe it is best to have a one-to-one relationship, that is, to have each use case implemented by a logical subsystem. This is an attractive view for managers because it is easy to understand and easy to staff. You simply assign use cases to developers for implementation. This design approach is a version of functional decomposition. A lot of experience has shown that functional architectures are inelegant, with a lot of redundant code, and are hard to maintain and extend.

With object-oriented design, the relationship between use cases and logical components is subtler. In a robust architecture, each subsystem collaborates with others; each provides an easily understood service that is often more general than any use case. The architecture is complete when it can be shown that the subsystems can collaborate to carry out the use case. With this design approach, we say the subsystems *realize* the use cases. The relationship between use cases and subsystems is not one-to-one, but many-to-many. Each use case makes use of the services of several subsystems, and each subsystem participates in the realization of several use cases.

For example, there are several use cases for an automobile, such as accelerating, making a turn, and stopping. The making-a-turn use case must include a range of speeds and turning radii. The standard drive-train architecture for a rear-wheel-drive car consists of an engine, transmission, drive shaft, and differential. The differential allows the rear wheels to go at different speeds so that the car will not turn over on a curve. There is no user requirement for a differential; the car must remain upright. Staying upright might be achieved using different drive train architectures, such as two small engines, one for each rear wheel. This architecture undoubtedly has drawbacks in terms of weight and cost.

In this example, the ultimate requirement is for the car to operate safely. The components—engine, transmission, drive shaft, and drive train—collaborate to meet this requirement. There is also a requirement for electricity to be generated to drive the instruments, the internal network, the entertainment system, and so on. The electrical system includes the same engine as the drive train. There could be two engines, one to drive the car and one to charge the battery and provide electricity, but such a design is easily rejected. It makes more sense to design one engine that can power both the car and the alternator (and the air conditioner, the power steering, and so on). A one-to-one correspondence between the requirements and the components is not necessary in an automobile. It is also not necessary in your software.

The logical view is used to address the robustness, maintainability, and extendability of the system. Returning to the example given in Chapter 1, suppose your team presents a printer design that has 25 moving parts. The competitive product has only five moving parts. Your team claims that the bill of materials for the 25 parts costs less than the more integrated design the competition is using. Even so, you should have serious concerns. All of those moving parts are likely to result in reliability, maintainability, and extendibility problems. More parts interacting with each other mean more points of failure. The design will be hard to modify. In the end, the more elegant design may support a better overall business case. Remember that quality is free.

The analogy holds for software. Each part of the design (subsystem, package, and class) is analogous to a moving part. The fewer, the better. Even more important: The fewer the interactions, the better.

2.3.3 Collaboration Diagrams

As logical elements, the classes or subsystems need to be able to collaborate to carry out the use cases. Collaboration diagrams are the mechanism for capturing exactly how the logical elements work together to provide the needed functionality. There is more than one kind of collaboration diagram. An example of the most common, the *sequence diagram*, is shown in Figure 2-8. Generally, there is one diagram for a given use case scenario. The elements of the diagram are instances of the classes that participate in carrying out the use case and their interactions. In some cases, the diagrams show the invocations of the detailed class methods. Other times, such as in the example shown in Figure 2-8, the interactions are generic services provided by the classes or subsystems.

In Figure 2-8, each vertical line represents a subsystem. The flow of time is perceived by reading in the downward direction on the page. The messages are the arrows between the lines. The vertical ordering of the lines sequences the interactions.

Collaboration diagrams serve several important functions. Primarily, they are used to determine the adequacy of the logical design to carry out the use cases. In practice, the act of creating the sequence diagrams uncovers some needed, missing functionality in the class or subsystem design. Once discovered, this deficiency is easily corrected. The same discovery during system test of a built system would be more expensive to address. Another use of the diagrams is to balance the traffic. If the sequence diagram for a given use case results in a great deal of traffic between two logical elements, these program entities will hard to debug. The team should consider resetting and balancing their responsibilities.

2.3.4 Component View

As the logical design comes together, the team also needs to consider how the code will be built and delivered to the customer. These design decisions are captured in components diagrams. The components are the actual files that make up the application as it is delivered to the customer. They are all those files that you see being installed when you run the install scripts on your computer.

The component design is based on different concerns than the logical design. It is based on physical considerations such as the different hosting systems, the

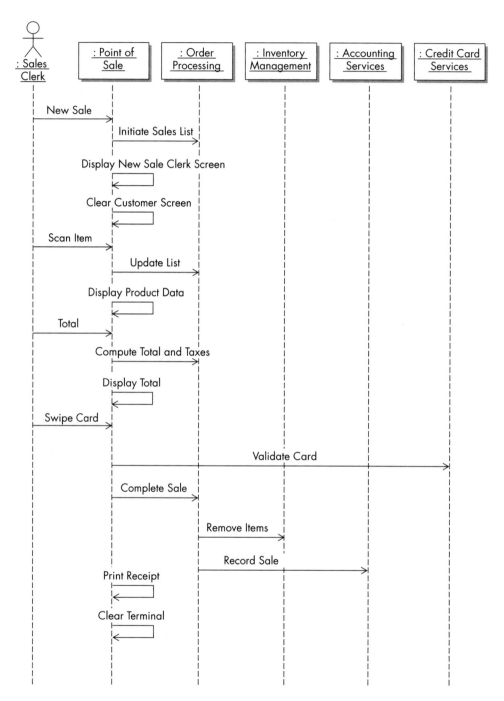

Figure 2-8 Sequence Diagram

memory used by the software, and the parts of the program that must run in parallel. Sometimes, but not always, subsystems are mapped directly into components. Although associating one subsystem with one component is the simplest solution, this approach may be impractical for several reasons. The result may be an executable file that is too large for the hosting computer, or the subsystem may need to be distributed across several computers.

Each component is determined by its classes. That is, the code associated with a set of classes is compiled together to make a component. A class can be and often is used in more than one component.

The components have *interfaces*, that is, ways in which one component can interact with the others. A component's interface is determined by the class interfaces for the containing classes. Your team might decide that some of the class interfaces are exposed as component interfaces. Careful design can result in components that can be used in more than one project.

The simplest applications have one component denoted by an .exe extension in Windows. The next-simplest component design is a one-to-one relationship, with each subsystem built as a component. Figure 2-9 is a component diagram for our retail system. In this example, there are four components: a cash register application CaReg.exe with a coupon-handling extension Coup.dll, a sales handling component, and an accounting component.

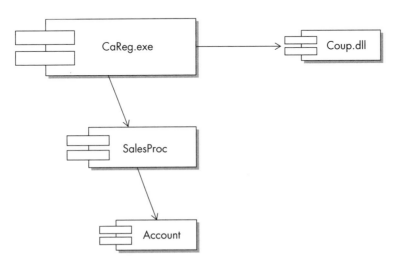

Figure 2-9 Component Diagram

2.3.5 Deployment View

The deployment view shows the physical relationship of the computers, their processors (for a multiprocessing system), and the networks that will host the applications. For much software, a conceptual deployment diagram, sometimes called a *descriptor node diagram* is appropriate. This shows the general layout of the physical resources without restricting choice to specific hardware.

An example of the deployment view is shown in Figure 2-10. In this example, the boxes are systems and the lines are network connections. In Figure 2-10, each store has a server connected to numerous point-of-sale terminals (modern cash registers). The store servers are connected to the corporate server. Note that the node architecture looks very different from the logical architecture.

The deployment view shows which components are hosted by which physical systems. For this reason, the deployment view is very useful in determining the

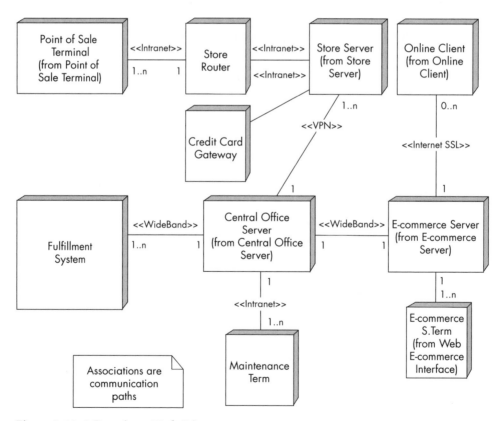

Figure 2-10 A Descriptor Node Diagram

component view. The deployment view is used to address issues like ease of installation and field maintenance.

2.4 QUALITY AGAIN

The purpose of the UML diagrams is to provide a mechanism for addressing the quality issues discussed in Chapter 1. Using the views, the team can consider alternatives, capture decisions, and establish the intellectual property created during the development process. In the following, I review each of the kinds of quality discussed in Chapter 1 and show how they are addressed with UML diagrams.

2.4.1 Usability

Many of the usability issues are captured by the use cases. First, the functionality of the software—its adequacy for carrying out the intended purpose—is addressed by having the correct set of use cases. If the software needs to be able to do something to be useful, there must be a use case to document that functionality.

Use cases provide a second view into usability. The scenarios describe how the actor, often the user, will interact with the system. By inspecting the scenarios, the users and the teams can agree on how best to provide functionality to the user. Consider the following example. You are asked to develop a program that allows the users to create furniture layout diagrams. One of the features of the program is its ability to simply draw straight lines between two points. Figure 2-11a and Figure 2-11b provide two different scenarios for drawing a line. Which would you find preferable?

Developing a program with either of the ways of drawing a line would meet the requirement, "The system shall enable the user to draw a line." A program that uses the first method (Figure 2-11a) would be almost impossible to use and would not be acceptable to most users. A program using the method found in Figure 2-11b would be much more acceptable. It draws a line in fewer steps and takes less visual acuity. If a person needed to rely on the program to draw many lines, his or her productivity would be greatly affected by the choice of method. The observant reader may note that the Microsoft drawing tools use this method to draw a line.

It is important to realize that the prospective users can read the use cases early in the development cycle and provide guidance on the usability of the software when there is time to fix the problem. The alternative is to have the users test the software after it is developed and ready for the field. Correcting a usability problem at that point can be prohibitively expensive and time consuming.

Step	Actor	System
1	This use case starts when the actor clicks on the draw line icon.	The system changes the cursor to a line.
2	The actor pushes the right mouse button.	The system rotates the cursor line.
3	When the line is the right orientation, the actor releases the right mouse button.	The system stops rotating the line.
4	The actor moves the cursor so that it is centered between the endpoints of the line and then pushes the left mouse button.	The system draws a line with the same orientation as the cursor centered at the endpoint and changes the cursor back to the system default.
5	The actor moves the cursor over the line and pushes the left mouse button.	The system makes the line blink.
6	The actor pushes the right button or the left button.	If the right button is pushed, the system lengthens the line; if the left button is pushed, the system shortens the line.
7	This use case ends when the line is the correct length and the actor releases the button.	The system draws the line and stops the blinking.

Figure 2-11a A Use Case Description for an Inefficient Way of Drawing a Line

Step	Actor	System
1	This use case starts when the actor clicks on the draw line icon.	The system changes the cursor to a crosshair.
2	The actor moves the icon to one of the desired endpoints of the line and pushes, holds the left mouse button, and moves the cursor.	The system draws a line between the first endpoint and the cursor. The line moves with the cursor.
3	When the cursor is over the second desired endpoint, the actor releases the button.	The system draws the line between the two points and changes the cursor back to the system default.

Figure 2-11b A Use Case Description for an Efficient Way of Drawing a Line

2.4.2 Repairability

Recall that repairability has two dimensions: supportability, the ease of making changes in the field, and maintainability, the ease of isolating and removing defects. Architecturally they are approached differently.

Supportability is explicitly designed into the system. It is first approached by developing the service use cases. In service use cases, the actor represents the role of system support. In practice this role may be filled by the user or be the purchaser's IT department. The service use case describes exactly how the system support actor will apply updates and patches. For example, the use case scenario will specify whether the software will need to be halted during update and whether the update will require a reboot. Once these use cases are captured, the development team should account for them in the logical and component design. It has been my experience that less experienced teams neglect to consider supportability until late in the development effort. As the leader, be sure your team considers it along with functionality as they design the software. During reviews, ask to see the service use cases. Ask that the team demonstrate how the logical and component design supports the service use cases.

Maintainability, perhaps more subtle, is achieved by having clear, concise portioning of functionality in the logical view system. As discussed above, each logical element, whether it is a class or a subsystem, should provide a clear, well-understood service to the rest of the system. It is important that only one logical element provide this service. If this goal is met, the designers will easily be able to trace the defect to the offending logical element. If the design is poor, the defect will involve some subtle interaction of distributed bits of code and will be hard to sort out. Once the defect is found, in well-designed software, the fix is usually restricted to a class or two. Therefore, the fix rarely causes some unforeseen effect. In poor code, fixing one defect without good logical partitioning often introduces some unforeseen effect that is a new defect. In fact, a clear symptom of bad logical design is that removing one defect often causes another. Such code is called *brittle*; every time you touch it, it breaks. If you suspect your code is brittle, you need to go back to the logical design to address the problem.

In practice, maintainability is determined by the logical design. As a leader, you need to ensure that your team has the motivation and ability to develop a logical design adequate to meet this and other quality goals.

Even though evaluation of architectures is more of an art than a science, reviews of the architecture can be useful. You may want to employ a consultant who provides architecture assessments or you may wish to get internal reviews. In any case, you should ask for a personal review from your team. Ask the team to explain the roles and responsibilities of the logical design. If their presentation is too convoluted, you may have a problem and need to seek out some expert advice.

2.4.3 Robustness

Recall that a robust system is one that can be used beyond its initial requirements.

One dimension of robustness is *extendibility*, the ability to add new function to the code. Extendibility, like maintainability is achieved through elegant logical design. If the logical elements are well encapsulated, adding new function will consist of adding new elements and reusing the existing ones. The review of the logical design also addresses extendibility.

Avoid Functional Decomposition

There is an interesting paradox in software and system design. Building a system that too closely matches the requirements can lead to poor quality. A poor way to do design is to assign each of the functional requirements, the use cases, to different teams for implementation. This design and development approach, called *functional decomposition,* is still common in the system engineering community, although, even there, the practice is losing favor. The result of this approach is functional code and little else. The code is likely to be redundant, hard to maintain, and hard to extend. A better approach to building a quality system involves first finding a logical and component design that is adequate to meet the requirements and then refining it so that it meets the other quality attributes.

There is another dimension to robustness, how well it works under various configurations of customer equipment in the field. If your software is a memory-hog that crashes most systems or has a tendency to fill disk space with temporary data, it will rightly be seen as having low quality. These issues related to customer equipment are addressed by capturing the operational constraints on size and performance in the supplemental specs and ensuring that the design explicitly meets and exceeds them. For example, if your target configuration is a system with 128MB of memory, try not to use more than, say, 100MB for the operating system. Otherwise, some unforeseen event will push the system to the edge and your software will take the blame.

During the reviews, ask how each of the supplemental requirements is met in the design. Ask how close to edge is the implementation. If the answers do not make you comfortable, again get help.

2.4.4 Reliability

Reliability is achieved in two ways. The first and most common is through having low defect, well-tested software. All software should be subject to this discipline.

The second is by building reliability features such as redundancy and automated error detection and recovery into the design. These special techniques are employed by systems that require extraordinary reliability such as banking software or those that involve personal or public safety. If your software has these special needs, you should have personnel with software safety and reliability expertise on your teams. They should be able to explain how the design meets the particular needs for reliability of the application.

2.5 THE GUIDING PRINCIPLE: ARCHITECTURE FIRST

In a software development project, architecture is the basis of almost everything. This chapter has discussed how the architecture provides the views for addressing the various dimensions of quality. As upcoming chapters show:

- The software architecture is the basis for managing the complexity of the effort.

- The software architecture is the basis for partitioning the design effort and the implementation effort.

- The software architecture provides a basis for facilitating team communications.

- The software architecture is the best basis for estimating the development effort.

A project that has a sound architecture can recover from any setback. A project that does not have a sound architecture is constantly vulnerable to failure.

So what about testing? One might argue the way to ensure quality is to be sure that you have the right tests to verify the quality of your software project. The underlying assumption to this approach is that having the tests, the developers will surely develop the needed quality. In fact, testing organizations are often given the name quality assurance.

Testing is important. The tests need to be developed and run. However, one cannot test in quality. It needs to be designed into the product. By focusing on the architecture, you and your team will have an effective way of meeting the quality goals and addressing any shortfalls found in the testing.

As a manager, you must focus your team on coming to agreement on a sound architecture. The architecture may be high-level at first, with details evolving throughout the project. It must be maintained throughout the project lifecycle, preferably using a UML modeling tool. The UML model of the architecture is the central project artifact.

To Learn More

The UML standards may be found on the website maintained by the

- Object Management Group, www.omg.org.

For all of the IDEF standards, see

- www.idef.com

Nontechnical introductions to objects and their benefits may be found in

- Guttman, Michael and Jason R. Matthews. *The Object Revolution,* John Wiley, 1995.
- Taylor, David A. *Object Technology, Second Edition: A Manager's Guide,* Addison-Wesley, 1997.

Two straightforward overviews of UML are found in

- Page-Jones, Meilir. *Fundamentals of Object-Oriented Design in UML,* Addison-Wesley, 2000.
- Fowler, Martin and Kendall Scott. *UML Distilled* (2nd ed). *A Brief Guide to the Standard Object Modeling Language,* Addison-Wesley, 2000.

The definitive UML texts are

- Booch, Grady, James Rumbaugh, and Ivar Jacobson. *The Unified Modeling Language User Guide,* Addison-Wesley, 1999.
- Rumbaugh, James, Ivar Jacobson, and Grady Booch. *The Unified Modeling Language Reference Manual,* Addison-Wesley, 1999.

For a discussion on capturing software design as intellectual property, see

- Jacobson, Ivar, Martin Griss, and Patrik Jonsson. *Software Reuse: Architecture, Process, and Organization for Business Success,* Addison-Wesley, 1997.

The following provides a technical introduction to the use of UML in system design:

- Lee, Richard and William Tepfenhart. *UML and C++, A Practical Guide to Object-Oriented Development*, Prentice Hall, 1997.

Two good books on UML-based business modeling are

- Marshall, Chris. *Enterprise Modeling with UML: Designing Successful Software through Business Analysis*, Addison-Wesley, 2000.

- Eriksson, Hans-Erik and Magnus Penker. *Business Modeling in UML*, John Wiley, 2000.

For a solid explanation of Data Modeling in UML, see

- Muller, Robert J. *Database Design for Smarties, Using UML for Data Modeling*, Morgan Kaufman, 1999.

- Naiburg, Eric J. and Robert Maksimchuk, *UML for Database Design*, Addison-Wesley, 2001.

This text discusses how to use UML for real-time and embedded systems:

- Douglass, Bruce Powel. *Doing Hard Time: Developing Real-Time Systems with UML, Objects, Frameworks and Patterns*, Addison-Wesley, 1999.

Chapter 3

The Software Project

The first two chapters were about the software product; this chapter turns our attention to the software project. It introduces you to some powerful mental models for approaching software projects. By understanding and internalizing these models, you can develop good instincts for leading development efforts.

The first two chapters described the software product, its quality attributes and its specification. We now turn our attention to the way in which software is developed. This chapter is an investigation of the software project. All software development projects have certain essential characteristics. Software development can be seen in various perspectives:

- As an exercise in collaborative problem solving

- As a kind of product development

- As nonlinear, dominated by the interactions of the participants

What follows is an explanation of each of these perspectives on software development, along with their implications for leadership. By understanding and appreciating these characteristics, you will have a mental model of software development that will help you make the decisions as if by second nature.

3.1 THE DEVELOPMENT PROBLEM

The problem facing the development leader is the creation of quality software within a specified time and budget. We will call this the *development problem*. Recall, in Chapter 1, we defined quality as meeting the stakeholders' needs.

One traditional approach to solving the development problem is to create a detailed project plan. This plan has fixed content, schedule, and budget. Once the plan is developed, all efforts are directed towards meeting the plan. Much of the literature restricts its attention to this solution. In fact, at least one well-known consulting firm defines project success exactly in these terms.

However, this connect-the-dots approach to development is unrealistic. Generally, one does not have enough detailed information to solve the development problem using a fixed, detailed project plan. The requirements are not sufficiently enumerated or even understood, the design is yet to be discovered, the estimates are imprecise. Moreover, as we will see, projects are inherently unpredictable; attempting to hold to a highly detailed plan is futile. A more realistic approach to software development must be found.

We start our exploration of understanding how to solve the development problem by exploring problem solving in general.

Consider how you solve a mathematics word problem. First, you make sure that you understand the problem. You make sure you understand the assumptions and what constitutes a solution. Perhaps you draw a diagram or recast the problem using a formula.

Once you are comfortable that you have a sufficient understanding, you can decide how to approach the problem. You might realize that standard algebra can be applied or that the problem is similar to one you have solved before. As you try to apply your approach, you may realize that you are missing necessary data or that you must go back to enhance your understanding of the problem.

Then, when you are confident that you fully understand the problem and believe your approach will work, you implement the solution. With luck, your approach is viable. However, you may discover that your approach is problematic or may not work at all. In that case, you proceed to refine the approach or find an alternative.

Finally, you verify the implementation by checking to make sure your solution solves the original problem statement. If it does not, you check your work, reconsider your approach, and possibly even rethink your understanding of the problem.

No matter what problem you are solving, from developing a high-energy physics model to installing a home network, you go through the same four phases:

1. Understanding the problem

2. Finding an approach

3. Implementing the approach

4. Verifying the solution

In software development, the entire team needs to solve the development problem collectively. The team as a whole must go through the problem-solving stages. The leader must take his or her team through this process.

3.2 DEVELOPING PRODUCTS

Product development is the discipline of creating and bringing to market consumer or business products. This field also must deal with a problem that is like the development problem. The product development leadership must find a way to design and bring to market, in a timely and affordable way, a product that meets the stakeholders' needs. Going deeper, we find several similar challenges. The product and software development teams must

- Create an innovative, elegant design that addresses the requirements in some optimal way

- Understand and adopt the latest technology appropriately

- Determine and prioritize user needs while meeting schedule and budget limitations

- Deliver a quality product that will perform well in the field

- Lead a team to achieve a robust, expandable, maintainable design

- Coordinate the activities of multidisciplinary teams

- Integrate technical and marketing strategy

Product development managers are not particularly concerned with generating documents. Their management approach to product development is as a collaborative problem-solving exercise.

In addition, many product developers must worry about manufacturability, generally a small problem for software developers. Therefore, while a few of the details are different, the overall problems are the same. Software leaders can benefit from the lessons learned from the product development community.

3.2.1 Product Development Lifecycle

There is no official product development lifecycle. From the various references given at the end of the chapter, you will find the following product development lifecycle is typical. See, for example, Ulrich and Eppinger [2000].

- **Knowledge acquisition**—gaining an initial understanding of the problem

- **Concept development**—creating a design approach to meeting the market opportunity

- **Product engineering**—implementing the concept design and adjusting it as necessary, adding design details to complete a full, detailed specification

- **Pilot production**—building a functional model to verify the solution and addressing any unresolved manufacturability problems

This development lifecycle ends at acceptance by manufacturing. Final bugs may be ironed out during manufacturing ramp-up.

Note how well these phases of the product development lifecycle align with those of problem solving listed in the previous section. During the knowledge acquisition phase, team members do everything necessary to understand what needs to be developed. They may interview users, read marketing reports, and consult with the sales organization. They may meet with management to understand business needs and the marketing strategy. They may develop a competitive analysis and study the underlying technology. The outcome of this phase may be a business case, a product proposal, a vision document, or a requirements specification. In short, the team understands the problem to be solved. When the team thinks it knows enough about the product, it is ready to proceed to developing the conceptual design.

During the concept development phase, the approach to solving the problem is determined. The development team creates a high-level (low-detail) design of the new product. They may draw pictures, develop a virtual prototype on a computer, or create some sort of mock-up. In the auto industry, they build life-sized clay models. An equipment manufacturer may construct a case or cabinet showing dials and displays (the user interface). This mock-up is tested with marketing representatives or a customer group in the user community. Product features are continually re-evaluated, and tradeoffs are made among the market value, the development risk, and the manufacturing cost. During concept development, the team may also consider several alternative design approaches and the tradeoffs among them. The alternatives may be evaluated in terms of the design quality attributes (for example, robustness and maintainability) and other product issues (for example, manufacturability and the cost of the bill of materials). Each design alternative consists of a list of the major product components and how they interact. This phase ends when the team thinks it understands how it plans to shape the design and agrees on the major components.

During the product engineering phase, the team implements the conceptual design. It fleshes out the design details until a full, detailed specification is completed. They may farm out the component designs to different teams. The development team continues to build a series of prototypes that reflect the increasing detail in the design. Team members evaluate the prototypes with respect to quality and manufacturing concerns. For example, two components may not fit together well enough to permit assembly without frequent breakage, or one component may interfere with the replacement of another in the field. Based on these determinations, the component design may be updated, requiring a trip back to the drawing board. This phase ends when the team is comfortable that any remaining design problems can be uncovered only in pilot production.

Eventually, in pilot production a fully functional version of the product is built and ready for transition to manufacturing. In this phase, the team verifies that they have solved the development problem. During manufacturing ramp-up, the development team addresses the operational issues of construction and assembly in the factory setting. They may discover last minute glitches that require some redesign. This phase ends when the product is ready for full production.

Given that the problems faced by software and product development are so similar, it is reasonable to expect that software development should follow phases similar to those of product development. This similarity will be discussed in detail in Chapter 5.

3.2.2 Phases and Iterations

One of the salient features of product development is that as the team moves through the phases, much of the team's activity consists of building a series of product iterations. Each *iteration* is a version of the product. As the development goes from phase to phase, the product iterations become increasingly close to final design. In the concept development phase, the iterations serve to help understand the product requirements. They may be mock-ups of the product for market testing. For example, a medical instrument maker may develop a version of the instrument with all of the buttons and knobs and no internal electronics. This mock-up can be used to test out the industrial design with prospective users. Later iterations can be used as a proof-of-concept to test out the practicality of the conceptual design. The final iterations might be used to address reliability and manufacturability issues.

Product development provides some important lessons:

- The maturity of the overall product design is marked by completion of phases rather than by completion of documents.

- Development progress is attained through product design iterations.

- The overall design is tested on an ongoing basis.

- A continual focus on meeting stakeholder needs is maintained throughout all the phases.

- Throughout the process, attention is paid to adjusting the product features to address development and market risks.

To summarize, in product development, the team goes through the phases of problem solving by developing a series of product iterations. As we will see, this approach provides a good model for software development.

3.3 SOFTWARE PROJECTS ARE NONLINEAR

Common sense flows from a shared view of how the world works. As shared world views change, so does common sense. Examples of how common sense has changed over recent decades include attitudes toward gender and race, as well as how teams work together.

The old common sense about software development was that the process was linear. The common belief was that teams should be managed like machines, each member doing a highly structured task while working as much as possible in isolation. This approach, sometimes called *scientific management* [Accel-Team.Com, 2000], sprang from the implementation of the assembly line in the early twentieth century and peaked with time-and-motion research in the 1950s. In this mechanistic approach, each person in the business process did one job repeatedly and, presumably, expertly. When their task was complete, they passed the item to the next person in the process. No one worker needed the big picture; they just focused on their own task. Interactions were minimal and the result was exactly the sum of the tasks.

Although an assembly line is efficient at producing many identical items that meet rigorous specification, it was found to have important limitations. First, the mechanistic approach did not provide a means for discovering and addressing certain quality issues. Some defects arose from the coupling of the tasks, from how people work together. For example, suppose one person follows instructions in placing a part on an assembly line. The next person sees that to place his or her part, he or she must hammer it in, degrading the product. If the two workers could collaborate, they might find a way to place the first part so that the second part fits easily. Another problem with scientific management was that people did not like being treated like machines. This management approach resulted in an adversarial relationship with management. The history of labor relations in the auto industry illustrates the point.

Some people see a mechanistic approach to business processes as common sense. Each task must be done. Why not analyze each task in detail so it can be carried out in the most precise and repeatable way possible? The *waterfall* software development process is an example of this approach, and early literature on the waterfall process makes such claims. The problem is that this mechanistic approach makes a leap of faith: that the interaction between team members is as simple as handing off a part in an assembly line.

A consequence of this linear thinking is the belief that the process, not the skills of the individuals, is the dominant contributor to success. The leaders of organizations that adopted this approached invested heavily in corporate processes and their enforcement. Their belief was that if they hired staff to fill the process roles with limited skills, the process itself would magically lead the team to a solution to the development problem. They held to this belief even though the research of Boehm [Boehm, 1981, 2000] and others shows that staff skill is the dominant success factor.

In what follows, we will show that process is important but it is not a substitute for skill. The process must provide a means to enable the skilled staff to work better together. To understand the role of process, you first must understand how members of the team need to interact. Today, we understand that development teams act more like societies or ecosystems than assembly lines. Each member plays a role in the community. These roles, not the artifacts, determine the interactions. With the right kind of leadership, the team members can come together in unexpected, but functional, ways to solve the problem. The dynamics of societies is nonlinear.

 The old common sense was about control; the new common sense is about leadership.

3.3.1 Nonlinear Dynamic Systems

A system is *dynamic* if, for all practical purposes, it changes over time. A bridge may rust or experience metal fatigue, but it is more or less static. The stock market is dynamic; so is the marketplace. So is your software team: Every day, the people and the work are different.

A dynamic system is *nonlinear* if the response is not proportional to the input; that is, if small changes can lead to large reactions. Machines tend to be approximately linear; most real-life processes, including software development, are nonlinear.

To understand how a nonlinear system operates, consider the following thought experiment:

> An automobile is placed in an empty, uneven field. You are asked to set the steering and speed, and to add the right amount of fuel so that the car, unoccupied, will arrive and stop at a specified target.

On the first try, you point the car in the right direction, compute the necessary fuel, set the speed control, and release the car. The car is buffeted by the wind, affected by the slope and bumps in the field, thrown off track by a pothole, and misses the mark. You try again and again, making all sorts of adjustments, and the car repeatedly misses the target.

You decide to take a systematic approach to the problem by running a series of experiments. You build a data table of initial conditions for the car, including the starting position, the angle of the steering wheel, the amount of gas, and the initial velocity. You set up the car with each of the initial conditions, let it run, and track where it ends. With enough data, you hope to be able to find the right settings to have the car arrive at the target. You plan several runs with each of the settings and average the results. When you run the experiment, you are amazed to find there is no predictability. The car ends up somewhere wildly different each time, with differences so varied that the averages are not reliable.

Eventually, you realize that unless the field is bowl-shaped and the target is at the bottom, the goal is unachievable. There is no repeatability. You observe that just a little steering would make all the difference. You realize that the outcome is affected by nonlinear interactions: interactions internal to the automobile (suspension, tires, steering), as well as by the outside temperature, the shape of the field, the wind, and many other factors. Each time you run the experiment, these nonlinear interactions affect the outcome. Because the car running in the field involves the nonlinear interaction of all these variables, it is a nonlinear dynamic system.

Scientists and mathematicians have come to understand the nature of such complex systems as the car in the field. An area of study, often called chaos theory [Lewin, 1999; Kauffman, 1996], is used to explain systems that involve many interacting entities. Chaos theory has been applied to weather systems, the dynamics of the marketplace, the origin of life, and, for about a decade, business organizations.

Some fundamental principles describe how nonlinear systems work. They provide guidelines for effective management of complex organizations such as development organizations. Most nonlinear systems are in one of three states, each found in business organizations.

State 1. Chaotic: Unpredictable and unadaptable

The behavior of chaotic organizations is always changing. The workers' tasks change frequently, so no one is sure who is doing what or who is responsible for what. People come to work each day trying to find a way to move the project forward. Attempts to get things moving fail. Interactions generate friction, and there is no discernable progress.

In disorderly projects, under chaotic conditions, team members do not communicate. They are continually in each other's way, unsure of what their job is. They spend more time trying to coordinate their efforts than moving the project forward. This kind of internal friction generates heat and not light.

Staff members of chaotic projects are emotional in interviews. They usually complain that what they do does not meet their job description, that they do not get credit for their efforts, that their time is wasted in unproductive meetings, and that their management does not seem to have a clue about what is really going on.

State 2. Stable equilibrium: Predictable, but unadaptable

Systems in a stable equilibrium behave as the car would if the field were a bowl. No matter where you set the car in the field, the car winds up at the bottom, in a state of equilibrium. The outcome is always the same. These systems require a large amount of external energy to move them from equilibrium. To carry the metaphor further, moving them from their stable state for the long term is like carrying the car out of the bowl. Small changes will not achieve this result.

Some managers believe that a stable equilibrium is good for their organizations. They perform year after year, seemingly impervious to the world around them. Their groups are not only easy to manage; they are hard to damage, even by poor management.

Sounds good, but there is a serious downside to the equilibrium state. Such organizations are very difficult to change, like the car at the bottom of the bowl. When the pressure to change is on, they resist new behavior; when the pressure is off, they revert to old behavior. These organizations do not compete effectively when changes in mission or technology are necessary. There are many examples, such as organizations comfortable with 1960s mainframe-based development methods. Given the amount of change in our field, these stable organizations are doomed. However, organizations in stable equilibrium are the exception.

State 3. Edge of chaos: Unpredictable, but adaptable

For most real systems, small changes in initial states can result in very different results. No amount of precision and detail is enough to set these systems on a course to a predictable end. Unpredictable behavior is intrinsic to these systems and cannot be overcome.

There is a state that is not in equilibrium and not fully chaotic. When systems are in this state, without steering it is impossible to predict their future state from knowledge of the present, like the car in the uneven field. However, these unpredictable systems do respond to external influences, so that they can be influenced to achieve a useful purpose. In the automobile example, a little steering makes it easy to hit the mark.

Edge-of-chaos systems have several remarkable properties that form a basis for understanding how best to organize and lead complex enterprises such as software development organizations. The first property is that small changes have large effects. As with the car experiment, a small change in steering direction makes a big change in the car's eventual position. This property is a defining characteristic of edge-of-chaos systems. It follows that it is impossible to predict exactly how these systems will respond to a plan or a set of directives. In fact, the greater the detail, the greater the unpredictability.

Fortunately, these systems are manageable, if not controllable, as a result of perhaps their most remarkable property: They spontaneously organize themselves into apparently orderly systems that adapt to changes. However, for this to happen, the system must consist of independent entities with the freedom to interact. With this freedom, the entities create the necessary connections and communications paths. System order does not arise from being controlled, but instead by being *managed*. In fact, any attempt to apply control may result in the system becoming locked in a rigid equilibrium structure that cannot make the necessary connections to deal with a changing environment.

3.4 TEAMS AS DYNAMIC NONLINEAR SYSTEMS

Development teams are made up of interacting individuals with different perspectives who generally do what needs to be done to complete a project. There are designers and testers, people who understand the application technology, and experts in software technology. Each is important, with unique experience, perspective, and priorities; each has a role to play. Throughout the project they need to interact, to communicate, to raise and address issues. As the project proceeds, the nature of the interactions changes. Each individual's interactions combine to become the team behavior. The theory of dynamic systems applies to this collective behavior of a team performing a development project.

Individuals typically fill one or more roles on a development team.

- The project manager, or lead, develops and maintains the project plan, including cost and budget; prioritizes and schedules the content; staffs the project; and provides day-to-day leadership.

- The project architect looks after the overall design and associated quality issues. Responsibilities include maintaining the integrity of the UML views, especially the top-level logical decomposition, and the problem report database. Brooks [Brooks, 1995] and others (e.g., [Booch, 1995]) consider the architect a key team member.

- The business modeler models the business process that the system under development is intended to support.

- The project requirements analyst analyzes the business model and other user input to develop the requirements database, including use cases and supplemental requirements.

- The developer designs, implements, and tests individual object classes.

- The integrator or configuration management staff defines the project code library structure, instantiates the configuration management environment, designs and implements the method of compiling and integrating the code (the "make" files), and creates the builds for testing and delivery.

- The tester develops test plans, carries out system and component testing, and generates test and problem reports.

- The documentation writer creates the help file and the content of the user guide.

Large projects require partitioning into several development teams, with each team responsible for some number of logical subsystems. With the exception of the documentation writer, each role should be instantiated within each team and at the project level. For example, there should be a project architect and a team architect on each team. The project architect looks after the overall system design; a team architect looks after the design of the assigned subsystems. All of the architects should form a joint design team. This sort of structure enables the communications necessary to achieve a coherent design. The same rationale applies to the test staff and the project team managers.

The person in each role has primary responsibility for one or more development items. However, they cannot work in isolation; they must communicate with other team members to be effective.

3.4.1 Order and Team Communications

One distinguishing characteristic of a development project, as a dynamic system, is that the entities are people, neither machines nor chemical molecules. The emotions and motivations of the team members are among the conditions and variables that interact to govern their behavior. Applying leadership, you affect these variables and steer the project.

Several scientists have considered models of how systems of interacting discrete entities evolve [Kauffman, 1996; Lewin and Regine, 2000]. They have found that the nature of the system is determined by communications among the entities:

- If communications are too restricted, the system will be in a stable equilibrium.

- If communications among the entities are excessive, the system becomes chaotic.

- A middle range is optimal. With just enough communications, the system is at the edge of chaos and evolves stable, manageable structures.

The following observations about communications are directly applicable to project teams, which consist of independent, interacting entities.

- When a team is too restricted in its communications, it does not have the means to adjust to the challenges of a development project. This can happen if the manager insists on being in all of the communication paths.

- If communications are unstructured, the project is likely to become chaotic. This can happen if the manager is uninvolved and the team must organize itself.

- One of the critical management tasks is to develop an organization that enables and promotes the right amount of communications.

This observation reinforces the wisdom of Brooks [Brooks, 1995] and others:

Tip　The key to leading successful projects is the right amount of communications.

This idea is entirely consistent with the software development economics model discussed in Chapter 4.

This new common sense provides a final insight: The global behavior of a nonlinear interacting system emerges from the totality of local interactions. It follows that you cannot mandate how your team will behave, but you can influence its behavior by the nature of your communications with team members. Think of this kind of communications as constructive involvement. Being a part of the team allows you to provide the necessary steering to keep the team focused on delivering the right product and to influence overall team performance.

Chapter 6 discusses some mechanisms for enabling the correct amount of communications and participating constructively in team efforts.

3.5 THE PROJECT PLAN

The automobile thought experiment is applicable in several ways to software development. In the thought experiment, the goal is to have the car arrive on a target; in software development, the goal is to have your team deliver a solution to the development problem. The initial conditions in the auto experiment are the setting of the steering wheel and the amount of gas in the tank; in the development problem, the initial conditions are the staff on board and their understanding of the requirements.

Note that a classic project plan pictured in project management books and supported by project planning tools is a linear object. It breaks the work into small pieces and adds them together to determine the effort and schedule. It does not account for the nonlinear nature of the interactions among the team members. As linear objects, these project plans are only approximations of what will take place. The plans then are useful only if they are not taken too seriously. As with many linear objects, a project plan can serve as a useful approximation.

Project plans are also predictions of the future. They contain information on what each of the staff members will be doing when solving the problem. Insights from chaos theory tell us that the information contained in a real-life project plan is unknowable. Insisting that a team hold to a frozen plan ignores the fundamental nonlinearity of the process. In fact, you can be sure that the initial plan is almost certainly not accurate. This does not mean you should not have a plan, but only that you must refine and update the plan continually throughout the development.

This process of refinement and updating enables the plan to serve as a steering mechanism. This requires the plan's details to be filled in as the project evolves. The team's experience in a given phase serves as input to the details of the plan for the next phase. This iterative development of the project plan is one of the features of the Rational Unified Process, introduced in Chapter 5.

3.5.1 Less Is More

Some managers and staff process engineers do not understand the nonlinear nature of their projects. They believe that the reason project plans aren't followed is that they are not sufficiently detailed. They believe that adding granularity to a project plan creates order. (Adding *granularity* means adding tasks of a shorter duration.) For example, the manager may respond to an identified shortcoming in a previous project by adding more work items. Of course, more detail only makes things worse. Adding details takes the leap of faith that one can predict the future with great fidelity.

I have seen six-month projects with 1,800 work items. Based on 180 working hours in a month, each item, on average, would be less than two hours in duration. Anyone trying to administer such a plan would spend considerable time just updating status. Each developer from hour to hour would have to report which of the work items was being addressed. Fortunately, most organizations wisely ignore managers or process groups that try to impose such plans. The downside is that the projects are left with no plan at all. Ironically, the attempt to impose order results in chaos.

3.6 APPROACHING DEVELOPMENT RISK

One way that people think about development projects is an exercise in risk management. Some consultants on risk management recommend that the team identify all of the possible risks, usually through some sort of brainstorming session, and then ensure the risks are mitigated. While understanding and addressing the risks of your project is important, it is best to have a more structured way of thinking about risks in your projects.

People can only think about seven things at a time [Miller, 1956]. Given the complexity of software development, it is important to focus on the right things. A useful way to identify and track the issues in managing a software project is to track a small number of development risks.

The literature on software risk analysis is extensive and typically overly elaborate: lists of hundreds of possible risks; bureaucratic procedures that consist of risk management plans, brainstorming sessions with risk identification, and periodic assessments. Most of this is wasted effort. In the spirit of keeping things simple, you should focus on the three project risks:

- Schedule risk: Not delivering the project on time

- Cost risk: Exceeding the budget before you deliver the project

- Quality risk: Delivering software that fails to meet stakeholder needs

Other so-called risk items such as staffing risk (the inability to staff) or technical risk (uncertainty about how to design the code) put the project at risk only to the extent that they affect schedule, cost, or quality. For example, the inability to staff is only a problem if it will put the schedule at risk.

3.6.1 Schedule Risk

The product development perspective addresses schedule risk in three ways:

1. It provides insight into the progress of the software development. By tracking the progress of the actual product and not trying to gauge completion of the activity, the manager can determine the true schedule variances. This accurate and timely insight enables the manager to address schedule risk.

2. It provides ongoing integrations and prototypes. Because this approach supports evolving versions of the software rather than integration at the end, technical risk is distributed throughout the effort rather than being stacked at the end.

3. It provides phases with planned milestones. Planned milestones provide momentum for completion of the effort. The defined phases with specified completion criteria allow the manager to keep the team focused on the dates. The phases help keep the project from spiraling out of control.

3.6.2 Cost Risk

The attributes of the product development perspective that help address schedule risk also apply to cost risk. In addition, the manager can prioritize content throughout the development. Iterations are planned so that the most essential features are addressed early. As development progresses, the manager can drop unessential features as necessary to hold to the budget, based on cost/benefit tradeoffs. In contrast, the systems engineering approach does not provide the mechanisms for making such tradeoffs once the specifications are written.

3.6.3 Quality Risk

The product development method addresses quality risk in several ways. The underlying approach is to find a solution to the development that satisfies the product needs. The manager can keep the team focused on the system architecture as the solution evolves. Finally, with good schedule and cost management, the team will not be scrambling to patch together a solution at the end of the project. They will have time to address the quality attributes.

The manager can review the software with stakeholders at each iteration of the evolving software. Necessary changes and tradeoffs can be made throughout the project. The product development approach does not rely on perfect knowledge and understanding at the beginning of the project.

3.7 A WORD OF CAUTION: NO SILVER BULLETS

The product approach may be a good framework for understanding system development, but it is not a silver bullet. Its application takes a significant investment from software managers: You must understand how to apply the approach in a detailed, disciplined way and lead your organization in adopting it. Fortunately, there is a detailed software methodology, the Unified Process, that provides the activities, phase specifications, and milestones needed to apply the product development approach to software. The Unified Process is discussed in Chapter 5.

There is a second type of investment for software managers: The success of the product development approach requires the ongoing involvement of all levels of management. This is a good thing. It is addressed in Chapter 6.

To Learn More

Here are some excellent references on product development. I most highly recommend the first reference.

- Ulrich, Karl and Steven Eppinger. *Product Design and Development*, McGraw Hill, 2000.

- Wheelwright, Steven C. and Kim B. Clark. *Revolutionizing Product Development*, The Free Press, 1992.

- Tabrizi, Behnam and Rick Walleigh. "Defining Next-Generation Products: An Inside Look," *Harvard Business Review*, November–December, 1997.

- Gorchels, Linda. *The Product Manager's Handbook*, NTC Business Books, 1995.

For over 20 years, Prof. Barry Boehm and his students at the University of Southern California have been studying software development productivity. The results of this effort may be found in

- Boehm, Barry. *Software Engineering Economics*, Prentice Hall, 1981.
- Boehm et al. *Software Cost Estimation with COCOMO II*, Prentice Hall, 2000.

Many who develop software believe that the chaotic nature of the field is due to its immaturity. These texts show the dynamics are much the same for more established fields.

- Sabbaugh, Karl. *A Jet for the New Century: The Making and Marketing of the Boeing 377*, Scribner, 1996.
- Sabbaugh, Karl. *Skyscraper: The Making of a Building*, Penguin, 1991.

Fred Brooks was the first author to document the nonlinear nature of software projects in this classic:

- Brooks, Frederick P., Jr. *The Mythical Man-Month* (Anniversary ed.), Addison-Wesley, 1995.

This is one of the first books to explore the management implications of object-oriented development. It has many good insights.

- Booch, Grady. *Object Solutions: Managing the Object-Oriented Project*, Addison-Wesley, 1996.

There have been several books for the layman on the nature of nonlinear systems. Three of my favorites are

- Bak, Per. *How Nature Works*, Copernicus, 1999.
- Kauffman, Stuart. *At Home in the Universe: The Search for Laws of Self Organization and Complexity,* Oxford University Press, 1996.
- Lewin, Roger. *Complexity: Life at the Edge of Chaos* (2nd ed.), University of Chicago Press, 1999.

One of the best books on the application of nonlinear dynamics to management is this recent text.

- Lewin, Roger and Birute Regine. *The Soul at Work: Listen, Respond, Let Go,* Simon & Schuster, 2000.

This is the classic paper on the limits of people's ability to process information. You will be able to find it online as well.

- Miller, George A. "The Magical Number Seven, Plus or Minus Two: Some Limits on Our Capacity for Processing Information," *Psychological Review*, *63*, 81–97, 1956.

At this writing, a summary of the history of scientific management may be found at

- Accel-Team.Com, Scientific Management. Lessons from Ancient History through the Industrial Revolution, online, http://www.accel-team.com/ scientific/index.html, 2000.

Chapter 4

Software Development Productivity

Even though software development is a nonlinear process, it is possible to model project efficiency. This chapter introduces a model and describes what guidance it provides for effective leadership.

In the last chapter, we established that software development projects are governed by the mathematical principles of nonlinear dynamic systems. As such, software projects have limited predictability; they cannot be managed by creating and stubbornly following detailed plans. Even so, there is much the leader can do to enhance the likelihood of project success. Some of those recommendations can be found in this and the following chapters.

Nonlinear systems may be unpredictable in detail, but they are governed by general rules that can be useful in managing overall system behavior. Consider the following simple experiment: Set up an apparatus that slowly, but steadily, releases a stream of sand over the same spot on a large table. Eventually, the sand builds into a pile. As the pile grows, every so often an avalanche will occur; some of the sand will break loose from the pile and fall down hill. Imagine you have some way of measuring the size of the avalanches, that is, the amount of falling sand. Even though the actual time between avalanches is entirely unpredictable, the fact that there will be avalanches is entirely predictable. As you track the number and size of the avalanches, you find that there is a predictable relationship between an avalanche's size and frequency over the course of the experiment. It is not surprising that large avalanches are less frequent than small ones. What might be surprising is that real experiments have shown that the graph of the relationship between the number n of the avalanches of a given size s always falls on an exponential curve, $n = s^{-b}$. Avalanches are unpredictable in principle; you can never be sure when the next avalanche will occur. However, you can be sure there will be avalanches and there will be many small ones and just a few big ones. For a discussion of real avalanche experiments, see Bak [1996].

Software projects are in some ways similar to our avalanche experiment. If left to their devices, software projects are unpredictable in detail. However, there are general underlying principles that predict how the projects behave. These principles give the project leader a means to affect the project's outcome, to enhance the likelihood of success. Many of the principles are summarized in the *software development economics model*, which describes the factors that make up a project's productivity. This model and its implications for software leadership are described in this chapter.

4.1 THE SOFTWARE DEVELOPMENT ECONOMICS MODEL

For most projects, labor is the major expense; minimizing labor usually results in minimizing expense. In 1998, Walker Royce [Royce, 1998], leveraging the work of USC Professor Barry Boehm and his students, introduced a conceptual model for the effort required to develop software. This model serves as a valuable guide to improving software development productivity:

$$effort = (team)(tools)(complexity)^{process}$$

where:

- *effort* is the manpower or cost. It is measured in programmer-months or equivalent.

- *team* is the amount of challenge the project places on the organization, mainly as a result of team inexperience, the innovation required of the developers, or the number of special requirements placed on the software. Sources of team difficulty may include required software reliability, constraints on performance and storage, required reuse of developed components, and team experience with the programming environment.

- *tools* is the efficiency gained or lost due to the level of process automation. More tool automation lowers the tools factor, thereby lowering the effort and improving efficiency.

- *complexity* is the effort associated with the amount of material to be generated by the team. Although complexity in this context is often associated with the number of lines of code, it should also include all other materials to be generated such as documentation, test cases, and training materials.

- *process* measures the gain or loss in productivity caused by team interaction. Generally, it is tied to the amount of interaction required of the developers. A high level of interaction is inefficient; time is spent coordinating activities, not generating software. If everyone can work as independent entities, process = 1. This value is a good approximation for small projects with one to three developers. If there is a loss of efficiency due to interactions, process > 1. In a very inefficient organization, if changing code involves everyone having to talk with everyone else, process = 2. In this case, doubling the amount of code increases project effort by a factor of 4. If there are efficiencies in the environment that allow one developer to benefit from the effort of another, process < 1. Typical projects have process factors between 1 and 1.5.

   Note that productivity is inversely proportional to effort, and so anything the leader can do to lower the terms in the equation will improve productivity.

COCOMO II

The software development economics model is a generalization of the COCOMO model developed by Barry Boehm and his students at the University of Southern California [Boehm et al., 2000]. COCOMO II and its variants provide accurate estimates of the effort required by a particular organization to carry out a particular project. These models can also be used to plan staffing and schedule. To use the model, the user must provide values for difficulty and interactions for various types of projects, or provide a framework for calibrating the organization (finding the parameters that fit the organization), or both. In a survey of the model's effectiveness, its predictions were within 30% of the actual values for roughly 80% of the projects.

For our purposes, you can treat the equation and its factors not as a precise mathematical expression, but rather as a summary of the contributors to development effort and their relationship. The form of the equation reinforces the nonlinear nature of software development. In particular, note that the factors multiply, with the exception of *process,* which is an exponent. Because of the form of the equation, changing any one the factors can have a profound effect on productivity. For example, halving the *team* variable alone can double productivity. One lesson learned from the model is that as an exponent, the *process* variable can have the greatest effect. Small changes in that variable can have huge effects, so the leader must pay particular attention to choosing an efficient process. Some readers might recall that exponential nature of the productivity model due to the challenges is one the main insights of Fred Brooks in *The Mythical Man-Month* [Brooks, 1995]. He too discovered that interteam communications had an exponential effect on productivity.

The model tells us that there are four ways you can affect software development efficiency:

- Managing the project difficulty

- Reducing the size of the effort

- Improving the efficiency of the organization

- Automating routine tasks

Let's explore each in turn.

4.2 MANAGING THE PROJECT DIFFICULTY

Project difficulty is a relative thing; what is difficult for some teams is easy for others. The best way to manage difficulty is to hire and retain a staff for whom problems are easy. The more competent your staff, the less difficult the task. This point cannot be overstated. Early research has shown that, overwhelmingly, the major contributor to a team's productivity is staff competence. See, for example, Boehm [1981].

It is easy to see that software development managers focus solely on staffing. They take the software-as-craft approach discussed in the appendix: They hire the best people and get out of their way. In the real world, not every organization can hire the best people.

4.2.1 Hire and Train

In my experience, you can rarely find just the people with exactly the skills you need. You will have to hire generally talented developers and provide the opportunity and training to develop the needed program skills. It follows that training your staff is an essential investment, but the training must be timely and appropriate.

As any project begins, it is wise to audit the staff's skills in the following areas:

- **Domain knowledge**—the particular development techniques of the system. For example, business applications writers and real-time telecommunications switch developers have different domain knowledge.

- **Development knowledge**—expertise in design and programming language specification. Development knowledge should include UML and the language to be used for development, such as C++, Java, or XML.

- **Environment knowledge**—proficiency in the tools and process to be used on the project.

- **Role knowledge**—proficiency in the particular skills needed to carry out each person's team role, such as architecture or testing.

If there are skill deficits, the manager has a decision to make: Ignore the problem and hope that the staff will learn on the job, or provide the needed training. The second choice is usually more efficient, especially if you provide just the training the team members need to carry out their immediate assignment. By providing the training in a just-in-time manner, you can be sure the training dollars are spent wisely. Risk will be taken from the project and the team will benefit by the training by having it reinforced by project activity.

4.2.2 Limit Innovation

Innovation can stem from developing an entirely new application, or developing a familiar application on a new platform, or both. The worst case is when an organization needs to develop a new application that must run on a new piece of hardware using a new operating system. Sometimes this situation is inevitable, such as when a team is programming a new telecommunications switch to meet a new communications standard. The number of uncertainties that the team faces in such a situation is extraordinary, making the development problem very difficult.

The manager should be aware of the sources of innovation and try to limit them, if possible. For example, if the team members must develop a new application on a new platform, they should build a familiar application on the new platform first, if they have time. Then they would be familiar enough with the new platform to try the new application. If there is no way to address the problem, effort will probably be high and productivity low. In this case, make allowances in your plan and budget.

4.2.3 Simplify the Effort

Once you have a method for ensuring your team is developing the right material, you are faced with finding a way to simplify the material development. Some approaches to developing the material can add effort and risk to your program; some methods can reduce efforts and expense. This section provides some ideas on how to find the simpler way.

Break Big Problems into Small Problems Try this experiment: Shuffle a deck of 52 cards and sort them by suit, from deuce to ace. Do this by going through the deck and finding the 2 of clubs and moving it to the front of the deck, then finding the 3 of clubs and moving it immediately behind the 2 of clubs, and so on. This is a tedious task. Now shuffle again and divide the deck into four piles. Put the cards in each pile in order by suit and number as before. Note that sorting the four smaller decks is much less tedious than sorting the full deck. Now merge the piles into one sorted deck by going through the piles and picking the cards you need. This is easy because each pile is already in order. One can prove mathematically that the second method takes less effort than the first [Knuth, 1998]. The reason the second method takes less effort is that there are fewer interactions required between cards, fewer comparisons to be made.

The best way to deal with a complex problem is to divide and conquer, as in the card-sorting example: Break the big problem into a set of smaller, simpler problems, as shown in Figure 4-1. In that figure, there are 11 circles on both sides of the arrow. On the left, each circle is connected to every other circle. On the right, the connections are managed though a hierarchical structure. If the circles were code blocks and the connections code paths, it should be clear that the system on the left would be a disaster. If the circles were team members and the lines were needed conversations, the team on the left would get nothing done. As a leader you should keep this picture in mind and strive to model your problems to look like the right side of the diagram whenever possible.

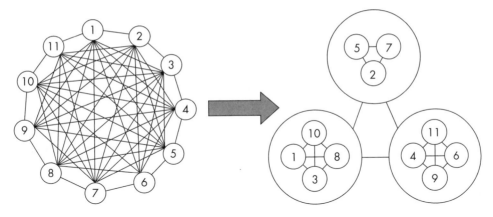

Figure 4-1 Hierarchy Defeats Complexity and Limits Interactions

Modern software development methodology provides two techniques for dividing hard problems into simpler problems: (1) adopting object technology, and (2) adopting incremental development.

Adopt Object Technology   Product complexity is a source of difficulty for most software projects. One source of complexity is the large number of system variables. A bug is caused if any of these variables has an improper value. As the code gets larger, it is increasingily difficult for the team to understand what path the code took that resulted in an improper value. Although use of code debugging tools helps, debugging a complex piece of code can still be very time consuming. For complex code, bugs are more likely, harder to find, and harder to remove. As in the card example, dealing with complex code requires the developer to deal with more interactions than necessary.

Objects allow the developers to apply the divide-and-conquer strategy from our sorting example. Using object technology, developers can sort the variables into classes, and the classes into subsystems. Further, they can limit the ways in which the variables can interact. In this way, the architecture itself breaks the big problem into smaller, more manageable problems. Like the card-sorting example, this approach takes less effort. An added advantage of this approach is that the subsystems can be assigned to separate teams, creating both concurrency and efficiency and reducing the schedule. This point is explored in Chapter 6.

Adopt Incremental Development   *Incremental development* is sometimes called "build a little, test a little." With this technique, the team first builds a small program with just some of the needed functionality. This small code is debugged, which is usually an easy task. Then more code is added to the program and the slightly larger code is debugged. The bugs in the new code are relatively easy to find because they are restricted to the new code or some interaction of the old code with the new code. These increments continue until the code is complete.

The alternative, sometimes called big-bang integration, involves bringing all of the code together at once. This remnant of the construction management mentality is based on the following assumption: If each developer has met the software specifications without flaw (like construction workers following the blueprints), the code can be integrated at the end of the development phase without difficulty. The number of unexpected problems during integration invariably surprises new managers who use big-bang integration. Experienced managers just gird themselves for the bad news.

Do Not Serialize Activities   Some software development teams do serialize and freeze the development of the artifacts. In a *serialized process*, first, the activities are often carried out by separate teams. The requirements team creates a perfect set of requirements, often captured in a document. This document is published and distributed. The designers analyze the requirements and create a design, which is once again published in a document. The design is used by the implementers to generate the code. The testers receive the finished code and test it prior to shipping. The process has a set of reviews to ensure the design meets the requirements and the code meets the design.

Serialization may seem simple to manage. First do one thing and then another. Don't waste effort on design until you have the requirements correct and so on. Nevertheless, serialization usually fails in practice because it requires the teams to do something that is humanly impossible: to get all of the details correct.

Software programs are too complex to try to get the details of any one artifact entirely correct without some amount of experimentation. If you ask your team to do the impossible, they will expend a great deal of effort trying. In the end, most teams will run out of time and declare victory, freezing flawed artifacts. This leads to a key characteristic of software development: The team can usually complete an activity artifact best while performing the next activity. The overlapping of activities permits the experimentation necessary to get the requirements or design or code correct without the team trying to do it all in their heads or on paper. The understanding of the requirements improves with the design effort, understanding of the design with the coding effort, and so on.

Serialization of activities is sometimes called the *waterfall process*. The waterfall process is discussed further in the appendix. In 1996, The Software Technology Support Center (STSC) of the United States Air Force published two volumes of articles to aid its staff in acquiring large software systems [Software Technology Support Center, 1996]. Vol. I, 3–22 contains the following advice in bold type, "In general, the waterfall method itself is NOT recommended for major software-intensive acquisition programs…".

Apply the 80/20 Rule.   As a leader, you might find the waterfall process attractive. It is easy to understand and seems to be easy to manage. However, decades of experience have shown that the waterfall, serialized approach is likely to fail. The problem with the method is that it does not reflect the problem-solving, nonlinear nature of software development projects discussed in the previous chapter. The team needs to create the artifacts in parallel as their understanding of the development deepens.

The *80/20 rule* explains further why the serialization of activities adds cost and risk:

> The first 80% of the value of an activity is achieved by 20% of the effort, and the last 20% of the value requires 80% of the effort.

This rule is a generalization of an observation made by the political economist Vilfredo Pareto (1848–1923) that about 80% of the wealth in most countries was consistently controlled by about 20% of the people. Koch has written an excellent treatment of how Pareto's principle applies to management [Koch, 1998].

The rule implies that it takes four times more effort to progress from 80% to 100% completion of any artifact than it took to get to 80%. Another way to look at this rule is that your team will spend 80% of the time being 80% done. If, because of serialization of activities, all they are doing is completing an artifact during this 80%, productivity will plummet. Because things change along the way, expending the resources solely to complete the artifact is a bad investment.

Fortunately, there is a way around this problem. The last 20% is difficult because the team needs more information about the way the system will perform. This information is found through design, building prototypes, and possibly reviewing them with users. If design and coding occur along with requirements specification, the project takes less effort overall. Movement towards solving the development problem halts while the team wrestles with details that are better addressed later.

Understand and apply the 80/20 rule.

4.3 REDUCING THE SIZE OF THE EFFORT

It stands to reason that a solution to the development problem with the least amount of newly developed material is preferable. This section describes how to minimize the size of the development effort.

4.3.1 Limit Product Functionality

Most software products have many possible features. Some are critical to the product; some are nice to have; some are extraneous. There is usually pressure to add functionality. Customers or your marketing people have wish lists that grow over time. Your developers come up with clever features that they beg to have included. Many project managers find that their projects grow in functionality over the development cycle. This is called requirements creep. Often, these extra features do not add stakeholder benefits in proportion to their effort. Each feature you include lowers productivity. As a leader, you need to ensure that your project team is carefully managing requirements to build in the right features and arrest creep.

4.3.2 Deliver the Functionality with Less Code

A second way to do less is to deliver the required functionality with less code. Some software designs are more elegant than others. A well-architected software system will generally meet the given set of requirements with less code than a poorly designed system. Poorly designed software tends to duplicate functionality across subsystems. For example, there might be three different subsystems for storing data, when one would do. This could happen if there are several functional areas in the system that need to store data. Each functional area builds a database with all the access and reporting methods rather than sharing a common code base. More code is written than necessary and productivity suffers. I know of a large, mission-critical government system that has three separate databases with identical data. Each database supports a different subsystem. Not only was the development cost higher than necessary, the ongoing expense of maintaining the three databases and ensuring they are consistent has proven crippling to the program.

4.3.3 Consider Code Reuse

Another way to do less is to incorporate previously developed, or off-the-shelf, code. On the surface, picking up and reusing existing code rather than developing new code seems reasonable. The preexisting code may be priced well below the development cost or may even be free of charge. Presumably, it would be debugged, removing risk. However, although it makes sense to use preexisting code in most cases, an unsophisticated leader can be unpleasantly surprised by the associated costs and difficulties. There are many factors to consider when contemplating reuse, including the source of the code, the level of the code, the risk, and, as a subfactor in all these considerations, the cost. However, several considerations can affect its actual cost, such as its quality, whether it is well documented, who maintains it, and whether it can be extended to provide future functionality. Nothing is free.

Why Reuse Efforts Often Fail

Reusing internal code may seem optimal because it may be free of charge. Over the past few years, leaders of software organizations realized that they tend to develop the same or similar code repeatedly. To become more productive and competitive, they invested in repositories for their internally developed code and they directed projects to reuse code whenever possible. Sometimes they required every project to develop and implement a reuse plan and assigned staff to conduct reuse audits to make sure the corporate reuse policy was followed.

In almost every case, these efforts resulted in little or no reuse of internal code between projects. Most reuse efforts have since been abandoned. Here's why.

For code to be reusable, it must be developed with reuse in mind. The code must have carefully defined, documented, flexible interfaces. Considerable effort is required to make the code reusable. Most project managers were not willing to expend this effort because they saw that it would add unacceptable risk and cost to their projects. The result was often repositories full of barely usable code.

Sometimes project teams searching the repository found code that was close to what they wanted but did not exactly meet their needs. Sometimes they could not tell whether it would meet their needs. Further, the candidate reuse code may have had an interface that did not mesh well with other candidate reuse code. In the end, the effort spent locating existing code, determining whether it would meet their needs, and modifying it was comparable to building new code from scratch. Software managers realized that the time spent trying to reuse code was often better spent developing what is needed. In the end, most reuse programs have little payback at the corporate level and can make an organization less competitive.

Finally, reusing existing code can be risky. The code may not work as advertised or, for some subtle, unanticipated reason, may not work as needed. If this occurs, you could take one of three courses of action, depending on the circumstances:

1. Fix the code if you can, if your team has access to it. If your team had also developed the source code, they might be able to fix it easily. If not, fixing the code might be a time-consuming, unplanned effort that could derail your project.

2. Work around the problem. If your team does not have access to the source code or if access is too difficult, the next option is to figure out how to use the code as-is by working around the problem. This usually involves some redesign and some compromise in functionality. This is a very common approach because many developers are good at finding ways to work around a problem. However, the impacts on schedule and acceptability of the final product are often hard to predict.

3. Beg for help. If there is no way to work around the problem, your project is at the mercy of the code provider. You are reduced to cajoling the provider to fix the problem or abandoning the code. This happens surprisingly often.

In summary, there are always costs associated with reusing code. The decision to adopt any piece of code should be based on a careful assessment of actual costs and effort. Sources of expense can include the design effort necessary to accommodate the code's interfaces, training, other ramp-up costs, and licensing costs, which vary from a one-time charge to a charge for each copy of the resulting code.

4.3.4 Reuse Architecture

Even though code reuse is problematic, architectural reuse is often very effective. Architectures, described in Chapter 2, are more readily understood and altered than code modules. Using a baseline architecture can reduce effort all through the development effort. However, effective architectural reuse requires a level of sophistication not often found in software development organizations. Those that do develop the sophistication will have a definite advantage.

Architectural reuse is an evolving practice. Some early articles on objects suggested that object classes would form a basis for reuse. This has not proven to be the case; objects are too granular. However, the recent literature suggests reusing larger design entities such as subsystems and components [Szyperski, 1998; Herzum and Sims, 2000]. However, reusing components can take significant effort. Because components are usually developed in isolation, their interfaces do not match. They are analogous to hardware components with holes that do not line up; they cannot be screwed together until some machining is performed. Invariably, new software must be developed to enable the reused components to work together. If the code to be reused has sufficient functionality, the effort expended in integrating the code is a good investment.

4.3.5 Eliminate Extraneous Material

Every project requires materials to be developed in addition to the code and architecture. Examples include test scripts and help files. Traditionally, development teams have used these documents to communicate with their stakeholders. Further, many development processes actually measure progress. Development processes often call for many development documents, including a system requirements specification, system architecture specifications, system design specifications, and interface control documents.

Many sophisticated leaders realize there are better ways to communicate than printing out reams of paper-based documents. Developers call this "killing trees." Even worse, in most cases the documents are out of date by the time they are printed. The documents invariably become shelfware once they are generated; they are put on a shelf and ignored forever. If the documents required do not add value to the project, they only lower productivity. Documents printed out on any two dates will not be consistent. If consistency matters, you have to freeze the content and so you are forced to serialize activities. It is important that all understand that only the development tool information, the database, is authoritative as a source of information.

Even with automation support, document generation can be a time-consuming, costly business: The formats need to be created or updated, some writing is usually necessary, and the output of the tool might need editing to ensure that document format is met. Every dollar spent generating the document is a dollar not spent on solving the real development problem.

It is imperative that your teams rigorously record requirements and designs. The key is that the information is important, not the documents. In fact, documents are an expensive way of capturing such information. Rather than generating documents, your teams should maintain the critical material they need on an ongoing basis in a database. All of the software requirements management tools, as well as architecture and design tools, are built on databases. Any documents based on the normal development artifacts are at best a snapshot and add no real value.

4.4 IMPROVING THE EFFICIENCY OF THE ORGANIZATION

Fred Brooks [Brooks, 1995] pointed out that the efficiency of a development project decreases with the number of people. This occurs because the number of possible interactions between the staff members grows nonlinearly with the number of people. If you have two people, there is only one possible interaction. If you have four people, there are six possible conversations; if you have 50 people, there are 1,225 possible interactions! This is a mythical man-month dilemma. Software projects of any size require enough people to get the work done in a timely manner, but adding people to a project will actually slow down the effort. A colleague of mine once pointed out that if you are adding a new person to a project, in order to get up to speed that person will tie up the time of a person who is currently productive. The net effect is two unproductive people. No wonder software development is seen as a dismal business. It follows that one key to effective software management is to manage team communications so as to keep inefficiency as low as possible. You need a way to add people while somehow maintaining productivity; this is the challenge of improving organization efficiency

Some key ideas of modern complexity theory are relevant here. There must be enough connectivity between the players (people communicating with each other) so that, as a whole, the team has a coherent view of the project. At the same time, if there is too much connectivity, the organization is swamped by communications. The key is to have just the right amount of communications to get everyone on the same page while maintaining progress.

You can increase organizational efficiency in several ways: by providing a development environment, investing in the architecture, building teams around the subsystem architecture, building the right product, and adopting and supporting UML.

4.4.1 Invest in the Architecture

How much should you invest in the architecture of the system? One implication of the software development economics model is that the architecture is free or even pays back more than is spent. The time and effort spent on architecture in the early phases of a development generally save more time and expense later, and they are certainly much less expensive and time consuming than trying to patch a bad design late in the process. Because the architecture unequivocally specifies the content and behavior of the system, it helps the designers and the customer make sure the system meets the customer's needs. Meetings become more productive, with less time spent revisiting decisions and trying to recapture decisions. Even more important, there is less breakage and rework due to poor communications.

Throughout my experience as a developer, I have come to realize that if my project's architecture is sound, then there will be always a way to overcome staffing and process challenges. If the architecture is flawed, no amount of process or management skill will save the project.

4.4.2 Build Teams around the Subsystem Architecture

The subsystem architecture provides a means for managing work, which has been divided among the subsystem development teams. This is a divide-and-conquer strategy. Each team works on the smaller problem of designing and implementing a subsystem. The coordination among teams is limited to specifying the subsystem interfaces. This strategy enables the manager to attain efficiency even for large projects.

Problem isolation and removal are ongoing activities throughout the later phases of the development. In a well-modeled subsystem architecture, the defects can be isolated to a single subsystem. This allows defects to be removed without creating new ones.

I have noticed a prevalent phenomenon among larger, more established organizations: Their architecture reflects their organization rather than the organization reflecting the architecture. This phenomenon results from the business having a large system in the field, one that was designed several years ago. That system was originally designed by a few smart engineers. Over time, the management built up an organization to maintain and extend the development of that system. The organization naturally reflected this older system's architecture. Management got into the habit of partitioning the work along organizational boundaries. Over time, the organization structure became so entrenched that the management could not imagine partitioning the work in any other manner. In most cases, they forgot how the organization evolved in the first place.

The existing organization that works well to maintain the old system is likely to be ineffective if the company needs to build a truly new system with a new architecture. This is the challenge faced by telecommunications companies going from voice circuits to packet switching or government agencies that need to leverage modern network-based computing environments. As a leader, you should evaluate your current organization's suitability to deal with the next generation of development. Let the new architecture be your guide. If you are successful, your successor will have the same problem in ten years.

4.4.3 Build the Right Product

Building the wrong product is the height of inefficiency. It is very disheartening if you hold to your budget and schedule and ship a well-tested product that fails to be acceptable in the field. The only way to mitigate this risk is not to hold to the original set of requirements but to adjust the content of the system to reflect current needs. New requirements may be discovered, market conditions might change, or the customer might develop a better understanding of what is needed. A mechanism is needed that enables the customer to review the product as it is developed to make sure it continues to meet the customer's needs. The best way to do this is to build the project in iterations and review the iterations with the customer.

Note that balance is required for this process. Changing requirements willy-nilly at every iteration will result in a failure to ship. On the other hand, stubbornly holding to the initial set of requirements often results in shipping the wrong product. Reaching the right balance takes leadership and discipline. At each iteration, revisit the evolving product with the stakeholders. As shown in Figure 4-2, sort out suggested changes in terms of two dimensions: *Value* to product and *impact* to schedule or budget. If a change falls into quadrant 1 (high value and low impact), then it should be adopted. Similarly, if it has high impact and low value (quadrant 3), it should be deferred, probably forever. If a change has low impact and low value (quadrant 4), consider it as "nice-to-have" and plan it for a later iteration. Either it ships or it doesn't. If a change has high impact and high value (quadrant 2), then some creative management is needed. You may decide to defer the change until shortly after the ship of the current product, or you may decide to replan the effort to accommodate the change. But you shouldn't accept the change without replanning the effort, hoping that somehow your team will come through. Unless you had a lot of reserve in your schedule, it is likely they won't.

The subsystem architecture provides a means for bringing discipline to these stakeholder-team interactions. The architecture enables the manager to determine the cost of the change by estimating the impact on each subsystem. Because

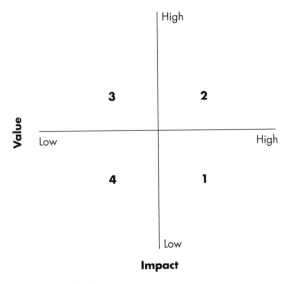

Figure 4-2 Change Evaluation Grid

requirements change, system modifications must be as efficient as possible. The logical decomposition underlying the subsystem architecture partitions is intended to be extendible. By partitioning the system into services that collaborate to meet the requirements, a change may often be restricted to just a few subsystems. This low impact is key to moving the project forward even when requirements change.

4.4.4 Adopt and Support UML

Modeling in any discipline is valuable only when it provides an efficient mechanism for unambiguously specifying a design to a wide range of reviewers over a length of time. For this reason, blueprints and electronic design schematics have standard syntax (symbols and their meaning) and semantics (definitions of how the symbols interact). Building codes formalize blueprint standards, and the IEEE maintains 12 standards relating to electrical diagrams. UML is the standard language for specifying software systems.

Many teams capture the system architecture using PowerPoint charts with no well-defined semantics, losing an opportunity to communicate what might be a great design. These models have only short-term value at best. Their ability to communicate is limited to discussions with the person who created them. Teams that present their designs this way will eventually have many unnecessary meetings to resolve their different understandings of the system because no one will be on the same page.

 Efficiency improves when everyone speaks the same language: UML.

4.5 AUTOMATING ROUTINE TASKS

As a software project develops, the team members create a variety of artifacts. *Artifacts* are any tangible item created in the course of the development. In addition to the delivered code and documentation, the team members should be maintaining lists of requirements, architectural views, source code files, test plans, and reports. All of these artifacts depend on each other. For them to have value, they have to be accurate and collectively consistent. Adding to the challenge is that different team members create, contribute to, inspect, and refer to the different artifacts.

There are two standard paradigms for capturing information: documents and databases. Documents are meant to be unchanging and static. Word processors and presentation tools generate documents. Databases are used to capture dynamic data—data that is expected to change frequently. An airline reservation system is an example of a database.

The document model goes hand-in-hand with serialization of activities. In a serialized project, the stable, static nature of documents is considered a plus. However, in a more iterative approach, the content of the artifacts is expected to change. Accordingly, the team needs to have a more flexible mechanism than documents to capture the architecture. For that reason, it is useful to think of software development artifacts as a sort of database.

Databases have features that help manage the accuracy, accessibility, and integrity of the contents. They provide efficient methods for entering and viewing the data. Databases can enforce rules as to who can read the information and the circumstances under which the information can be changed. Finally, elaborate databases can have mechanisms for ensuring that all of the data is consistent. If a piece of data is changed, then other data is likely to be affected. For example, changing a flight number can affect a passenger's reservations.

4.5.1 The Tool Environment

Software development tools provide mechanisms similar to those of database applications. They provide efficient ways for entering and viewing artifact information, and for maintaining consistency between the artifacts. A software development environment consists of

- **Requirements managers,** for maintaining the system and subsystem requirements and how they are related.

- **Architecture modelers,** for maintaining the various UML views and design information. These tools provide graphical interfaces so the developers can work directly with the UML diagrams. Further, they provide a mechanism for generated source code from the design. There are also real-time modeling tools that provide simulations of how the code will run in the target environment.

- **Test-case development tools** that use requirements as input and help create system test-case descriptions that confirm that the requirements are met.

- **Test automation** tools that execute the test cases and generate defect reports. There are also test coverage tools that show how much of the actual software is tested.

- **Configuration managers,** who keep track of versions of all of the artifacts and then through a labeling process provide a mechanism for associating the versions, the artifacts, and the delivered version of the system. Without this capability, large-scale development and field maintenance are almost impossible.

- **Defect and change request trackers** that allow any stakeholder to report problems or suggest changes to the system. These requests are maintained in a database. These tools allow one to define and enforce business rules as to how these changes should be processed. Examples of the rules might include a specification of who should review, approve, and assign approved changes to releases.

- **Code editors** that enable developers to directly maintain the source code created by the modeling tools.

- **Compilers and linkers,** who work in concert with the configuration managers in creating the executable software files for delivery to the users.

Note that the artifacts maintained by these tools are all related. The design and test tools depend on the requirements. The code depends on the design, and so on. In fact, these mutual dependencies provide a view of the overall challenge of team software development. Different team members must maintain the different artifacts, yet they must work together to have a unified approach. For the tools to be of the most value, they need to be integrated and provide mechanisms for keeping the artifacts aligned. In the end, the environment must support the goal that the artifacts document one product from many perspectives.

In summary, tools serve three roles in promoting efficiency:

- Automating the creation and maintenance of the artifacts

- Providing mechanisms for ensuring the consistency of the artifacts

- Providing a mechanism for tuning team communication

Automating Communications   A recurring notion in this book is that a primary task of the software development leader is to facilitate the right amount of communications among the team members. Development tools provide a mechanism for the leader to tune the formality of team communication. A team leader can put in place mechanisms for deciding both who and under what circumstance someone can enter or modify information and who can view it.

By using these controls with *change request* trackers, you can make the artifact changes as easy or difficult as appropriate for your particular project. For example, in large projects with hundreds of developers, you might want to create an environment in which a developer can update his or her part of the design with little fanfare, but cannot change any other part of the design. If the developer needs a change in some other part of the design, then he or she must generate a change request. Otherwise, the project will become chaotic. On the other hand, in a small project with a handful of developers, all of this formality is counterproductive, and it may make more sense to have the developers sit in the same room with open access to changes. The point is that the leader can decide exactly what is best for the project and even adjust the process to optimize communications.

Most development tools can generate documents containing artifact content. This capability is an advantage and also is another similarity to database applications. Databases come with report generators that provide the ability to create documents by publishing the data in some suitable format. To some, the use of development tools provides the best of both worlds; you get all of the advantages of the development tools and of documents.

Even so, I recommend that you keep documentation generation to a minimum. If you want to provide your stakeholders access to the information, rather than create documents for their review, you should provide them access to the real project information. For example, you can provide browsing capability of the project information maintained in a tool environment. This way the stakeholder can have timely, accurate information and your scarce development dollars are not spent generating documents with ephemeral value. You might find it of interest that, in my experience, even government customers, if given the opportunity, prefer browsing the real data to being given documents. In the same light, I hold project reviews with projectors connected to computers that have access to the real project information. I spend little time preparing for a project review; I just have the team present the real, working data.

Tip Use the development environment to optimize team communications.

4.6 ROUND-TRIP ENGINEERING

There is an important engineering principle: At any given time, a product should be built as designed and designed as built. This principle, sometimes called "round-trip engineering," means that a product and its design documentation should be entirely consistent. Otherwise, any further development or maintenance of the product will be haphazard, unpredictable, and difficult to manage. Round-trip engineering does not imply that the design should be frozen; only that it reflects reality.

Tip Code that is built as designed and designed as built results in an accurate system that is available for maintenance and development of the project.

Because of the complexity of software products, round-trip engineering is both important and challenging for software teams. Some software development leaders have tried to address the challenge of round-trip engineering by trying to serialize the development of the artifacts. Once created, if the artifacts do not change, they must be adhered to. Unfortunately, as discussed above, this tempting approach to maintaining the principle generally fails. The team needs some mechanisms to evolve the artifacts in parallel while keeping them synchronized.

In a modern software process, the team collaborates on the creation of the architecture. With UML modeling tools, code modules can be generated directly from the model. The degree to which the code generation can be automated depends on the nature of the application and the choice of tools. The code modules are grouped into libraries that are compiled into object code. The object code is linked to create the components that are loaded and run on the computer.

Traditional software management is focused on the creation of modules and components. Modern software management is focused on generating the architecture. This shift occurred when modeling tools that support automated code generation were adopted. Generally, the automatically generated modules are not complete. They contain the code skeleton, that is, all of the data structures and messaging interfaces required to be consistent with the model. The developer fills in the body of the module with the (typically) small amount of code that does the processing.

One consequence of automated code generation is that much of the work that previously went into coding can be done using UML modeling tools. Without modeling tools, the major source of error was often in the skeletons that are now generated automatically. Using the tools to design and then generate code is more efficient than using the model as a set of pictures, perhaps in PowerPoint, then going straight to code.

4.7 THE ROAD TO RUIN: MISUSING OVERTIME

I have left out one management technique: overtime. Faced with schedule pressure and the diseconomies of adding people to a project, some managers conclude that the answer lies in having their existing staff work more hours. Stories abound of programmers working 80+ hour work weeks for months at a time; inhuman work schedules for programmers have become a well-documented industry practice.

Having salaried employees work double shifts might seem like a great deal, with the project getting done at half the cost in half the time. Some managers create an organizational culture in which unreasonably long work days and weeks are the norm, where working fewer hours shows lack of support for teammates. Managers may even begin counting on unreasonable hours in their planning. When an original schedule slips, management may hold the developers to a set of milestones that require 16-hour days and seven-day weeks.

Counting on this sort of sustained effort usually does not work and, for several reasons, is very damaging to your organization in the long run:

- Difficulty grows. Working as a galley slave takes little thought, so it is hard to make a mistake when in that role. But programmers are not galley slaves; they need to think. Logical mistakes in their code can result in much wasted time. An employee can do only so much without sleep. The Bible tells us that people need one day of rest in seven. The more mentally exhausted the programmer, the more difficult the effort. As the model demonstrates, the overall effort increases as the difficulty increases.

- Efficiency falls. When workers are exhausted, communications suffer. Tempers are short and issues are magnified when people are tired or angry or both. Employees may be unpredictably absent just when they are needed, as they sneak out to take care of personal business they would normally conduct off-hours.

There are other pragmatic reasons not to fall into the excessive-hours trap. This risky strategy leaves you with no reserves when other problems arise. Team members working normal hours most of the time can pitch in for an occasional short-term push to make a critical milestone. This reserve is available if you have not squandered it by making excessive demands on your staff.

Expecting employees to work long hours as a matter of routine also results in low morale. Managers end up burning out their most valuable resource: their staff. No amount of tooling and process can make up for the loss of experienced, trained personnel. The manager may or may not make the first delivery through heroic efforts; however, the ability to make the next delivery may be diminished.

Finally, relying on excessive overtime is irresponsible and wrong, a kind of cheating. Managers who demand unreasonable hours are more like colonial plantation owners than modern industrial managers, exploiting their usually young staff. They are cheating their staff and their shareholders, and are failing to build value in their organizations.

A more reasonable alternative in the long run may be to operate two shifts. For example, it often makes sense to have some team members building and testing code at night and generating problem reports for the development staff to address during the day.

Tip To achieve competitive levels of productivity, a development organization must provide sustainable lifestyles for its staff.

To Learn More

Royce's model and its implications for project management may be found in

- Royce, Walker. *Software Project Management: A Unified Framework*, Addison-Wesley, 1998.

Royce's work is built on the research of Barry Boehm. This classic is still relevant.

- Boehm, Barry. *Software Engineering Economics*, Prentice Hall, 1981.

The COCOMO II model is explained in

- Boehm, Barry, et al. *Software Cost Estimation with COCOMO II*, Prentice Hall, 2000.

Everyone interested in software management should own and read

- Brooks, Fredrick P., Jr. *The Mythical Man-Month* (Anniversary ed.), Addison-Wesley, 1995.

The Air Force volume on software development is

- *Software Technology Support Center (STSC), Guidelines for Successful Acquisition and Management of Software-Intensive Systems*, version 2.0, Department of the Air Force, 1996.

These texts were used in the chapter's examples:

- Knuth, Donald E. *The Art of Computer Programming: Sorting and Searching*, vol. 3 (2nd ed.), Addison-Wesley, 1998.
- Bak, Per. *How Nature Works*, Copernicus, 1996.

This is an amusing and informative text on the 80/20 principle as a general phenomenon:

- Koch, Richard. *The 80/20 Principle: The Secret of Achieving More with Less*, Bantam Doubleday Dell Publications, 1998.

These insightful texts discuss the some of the technical aspects of reuse and why reuse of object classes fails:

- Szyperski, Clemens. *Component Software: Beyond Object-Oriented Programming*, Addison-Wesley, 1998.
- Herzum, Peter and Oliver Sims. *Business Component Factory*, John Wiley, 2000.

Chapter 5

The Rational Unified Process

This chapter introduces the development process that provides specific mechanisms to address the issues raised in the previous chapters. This process provides the framework for organizing, tracking, and managing the development effort.

Up to this point in the book, I have addressed different aspects of the software development problem. Chapter 1 introduced the stakeholders and their quality concerns. Chapter 2 described how quality can be achieved through software architecture. Chapters 3 and 4 provided insight into the dynamics of development teams and the economics principles that govern development principles. This chapter provides the means for solving the development problem; it describes a software process that can address all the issues raised in the earlier chapters.

The Rational Unified Process (RUP), developed by Philippe Kruchten, Walker Royce, Ivar Jacobson, Grady Booch, and others, is that process. It reflects the product-development, problem-solving nature of the work. It provides the means to achieve necessary balance between the disciplines to make and meet commitments to the stakeholders and the need for discovery of requirements and design details throughout the development cycle. Further, the RUP can be tailored to any software development effort: Web applications, large engineering systems, research prototypes, and so on.

There are several published versions of the RUP. Some of the versions are the Unified Process [Ambler and Constantine, 2000a; Ambler and Constantine 2000b; Ambler, Constantine, and Smith, 2000], the Unified Software Process [Jacobson et al., 1999], and Controlled Iterative Development [Cantor, 1998]. All of these versions share the fundamental principles and lifecycle of the RUP.

Perhaps because the RUP is so versatile, there is no cookbook to follow. Expertise is necessary to tailor the process to each organization and project. To apply the process, the software leader must first understand its principles and elements. This chapter describes those principles. It begins with a discussion of the issues that affect the choice of any software process. From there, it presents the elements of the Rational Unified Process, and discusses how these elements meet the criteria for a good software development process.

5.1 ADOPT A STANDARD PROCESS

Some software managers leave the choice of process to their project leaders. The project leaders may have convinced them that the project at hand is "different" and a standard process cannot be used. Although every project *is* different and some tailoring may be needed, a robust process should accommodate any project your team may face. If your technical team insists that your current standard process (if you have one) will not work for them, it is time to find a different process or possibly a different team.

Although every software project is different and some process tailoring may be needed, a robust process should accommodate any project your team may face.

Failure to adopt a standard development process will mean that each project is an adventure. Project teams will venture forth into uncharted waters—some filled with hope, some filled with dread. Teams will spend a lot of time looking for the route. They will need to decide what artifacts to develop and who does what task. The result will be frustration and internal friction. On every project, energy will be wasted learning new methods and arguing about processes.

If your organization adopts and follows a standard process, every project is a trip down a well-marked path. The team can get on with the journey, confident that they will not lose their way. If adjustments are needed, they are easily made without detours. Team energy will be spent moving the project forward, not generating friction. They can go from project to project with a clear understanding of artifacts to be generated, team roles to be filled, and how the work will proceed. Moreover, you will have a baseline for genuine process improvement.

5.2 GOOD AND BAD PROCESSES

Some processes are better than others. Choosing a bad process can do your organization more harm than good. For example, some bad software processes call on the staff to do the impossible: Serialize the activities by getting the design right, in full detail, before coding. Trying to manage your employees to an impossible process is a dehumanizing experience, for you and for them. A manager (a Texan) once told me, "Don't try to teach a pig to sing. It won't work and will only annoy the pig."

Well-known management consultant Edward Deming used the following exercise in his training seminars: "Workers" were given a large scoop and a bucket with a mixture of small red and blue beads. They were told to scoop out the blue beads and not the red ones. The objective was to get the number of red beads per scoop down to zero. "Managers" tracked the number of red beads on individual performance graphs, which were prominently displayed.

Although the managers tried to motivate their teams to improve, no amount of praising, threatening, or cajoling the workers had any effect. The variation in the number of red beads remained random. There is no human way to consistently scoop out only blue beads. Similarly, praising, threatening, or cajoling your staff to carry out an unworkable development process will have no effect. If the process is flawed, no amount of staff effort will have any substantial effect on the outcome.

Based on the material of the earlier chapters, a good software development process has the following attributes:

- Provides for the development of robust, quality code; in particular, treats the architecture as the primary artifact

- Follows the product development approach, treating the development as an exercise in collaborative problem solving

- Reflects the implications of the productivity model, with no extraneous artifacts

- Provides mechanisms for managing content, facilitating communications, and promoting staff efficiency

Further, a software development process should satisfy these five related requirements:

1. Problem Solving   As we discussed in Chapter 3, software development is a collaborative problem-solving exercise. This observation was confirmed by how the product development progresses. An effective software development process should reflect how people solve problems. A key feature of the Rational Unified Process is that its lifecycle phase aligns with the problem-solving phases described in Chapter 3.

2. Breadth, Then Depth   The Rational Unified Process accounts for evolving levels of understanding as the project proceeds. For this approach to work, the leader and the development team need to develop a shared view of the overall shape and boundaries of the project as soon as possible. This common view supports planning and prioritization of the effort and keeps development work focused.

In practice, this means that the team must prioritize the requirements and design work by documenting the breadth of the program. For example, it is more important to establish a complete list of requirements, based on the current understanding of the project, than to capture any of the requirements in full detail. Throughout the project, the Rational Unified Process requires the team to capture the broad outlines of the artifacts first, and fill in the details later. This applies to requirements, design, code, and even the project plan.

There are many advantages to this Rational Unified Process approach. Having broad requirements allows you to manage one of the primary dilemmas of software development: whether you are building the right program. Having the breadth of the design early allows for better apportionment of the work. Having an executing skeleton code early addresses architectural risk. In all instances, the details can be found with more certainty and less effort in the context of the broad outline.

Holding back a team from working on the details too soon requires management attention. This may be because working on details is easier than determining the broad outline. Engineers and programmers often feel more at ease working on details.

The same principle holds for the project plan. At the beginning of the project, you can capture the business commitments and major milestones. The detailed planning, such as the content of the iterations, cannot be planned until you gain a detailed understanding of the content. Your plan will be broad, with details to follow.

3. Iterative Development   Iterative development is a special case of the breadth-then-depth principle. It is central to the Rational Unified Process and deserves special attention. In the Rational Unified Process, the code is developed in a sequence of small incremental builds, each with more functionality than the last. The first build or two execute the broad outlines of the code. These builds confirm that the top level of the design works. In Rational Unified Process parlance, this is called developing an *executable architecture.* In the following builds, the functional requirements are delivered, a few in the early iterations and more later, until the code is functionally complete.

In practice, the team creates the first iteration by agreeing on a high-level design, implementing the code, testing, and debugging. This effort is followed by another round of design, coding, testing, and fixing defects. Each delivery has new functionality. The result of the entire set of iterations is fully functional, tested code. There is no test and integration phase. The final stage of the Rational Unified Process consists of making sure that the functional code will work in the customer environment.

The functionality of each iteration is planned. An *iteration plan* is the artifact that details the schedule and functional content of the iterations. Typically, because of uncertainties inherent in the development process, the iteration plan is updated continually throughout the project.

The iterative approach not only allows you to test the high-level design early; it provides a mechanism for staging the development of functionality. This allows the team to schedule development of the functionality, to address their view of the risks. For example, they can focus on the riskiest, most critical functions early and put off the nice-to-have functions until later. In this way, they can increase the likelihood of a successful delivery even if not all of the initially scoped functions are available by the shipment date.

There is another good reason for incremental development: The larger the code, the harder it is to debug. Building the code all at once and debugging during a test phase at the end of the project is the riskiest aspect of the waterfall process. Counting on a "big-bang" integration leads to fixing design problems at the end of the project when time pressure and expense are peaked. Building a small piece of code and debugging it, adding more code and debugging it, and so on, also takes less overall effort than building the code all at once and then debugging it.

An important benefit of the Rational Unified Process is that the risk of an unsuccessful delivery decreases steadily as the project advances. This fact does wonders for staff morale.

The iterative approach discussed here should not be confused with so-called spiral methods. With *spiral methods*, the entire application is built and shared with the user, and shortfalls and gaps are identified. These defects are addressed and the code is rebuilt. The code is again delivered to the customer for review. This process continues until either the code is accepted or everyone gives up in frustration. In my experience, the latter is the more typical result.

4. Objective Tracking   Another advantage of the Rational Unified Process iterative approach is that it enables objective tracking, so that development progress can be accurately assessed. With each iteration, the team demonstrates with testable, working code how much of the functionality has been addressed: Either a requirement is satisfied by the code or it is not. There is no need to guess if you are 21% or 32% or 43% done with the code. You are 32% done when 32% of the requirements have been successfully tested.

You can apply the same approach to other development artifacts. Once the breadth of the program has been determined, progress can be tracked by assessing how many of the requirements are fully detailed according to the plan and how many of the requirements are realized by the design. The processes discussed in the following sections provide objective measures for every phase of the development.

5. One Process   One implication of adopting the waterfall and its variants is that each software development activity (requirements capture, requirements, analysis, design, coding, testing planning, and so on) may be treated as a separate process. Each process is handled by a separate team, and its artifacts are handed off to the next team. This assembly-line mentality causes each team to own its own process in isolation. The result is that the organization practices a set of uncoupled development processes: requirements, analysis, design, and so on. In most cases, no one looks after the process as a whole.

The Rational Unified Process, based on iterative development, is a single, unified process. Hence its name. Each of the activities is designed to support the other so that the artifacts can evolve in parallel. To implement the Rational Unified Process, each of the development stakeholders has to adopt it as one team, each understanding the role he or she plays in the larger, overall process.

5.3 PROCESS ENGINEERING

The field of process engineering specifies how people perform work together. This section gives a brief overview of the elements of process engineering, with an emphasis on software processes. This overview sets the groundwork for comparing processes.

A development process is fully described by the following elements:

- **Phases:** the stages the project goes through from the initial idea to delivery. For example, the phases of the waterfall process are requirements specification, design, implementation, integration, and test.

- **Lifecycle:** usually a single pass through all the phases. A development can consist of several lifecycles.

- **Disciplines:** the functions your team performs to implement the process. Examples include design of the architecture, coding, and testing.

- **Artifacts:** the products developed in the course of carrying out the activities. Examples include code, use case specifications, UML models, requirement databases, and training materials.

- **Roles:** responsibilities that people assume in developing the artifacts and/or carrying out the activities. Workers are people who fulfill roles. A person may take on more than one role. A role can be shared by a team of workers.

- **Milestones:** an event that marks the completion of a development phase

- **Iterations:** the number of times the process calls for building and testing the code throughout the lifecycle

When you adopt a process, you and your team should have a clear understanding of each of these process elements.

5.4 ITERATIVE DEVELOPMENT

Building the code in an iterative manner in the Rational Unified Process has many advantages. The first is that it helps management by providing a mechanism for assessing real progress of the development. Either an iteration can exhibit a use case as planned or it cannot. If it cannot, there is a schedule slip. There is no room for argument. As a leader, you need to understand the recovery plan. You have an early indication of the schedule slip, which gives you the opportunity to uncover the cause and see whether you can help. The early notice enables you to be a constructive, involved member of the team.

The iterations also help the developers because the amount of code change from one iteration to the next is relatively small and easily understood. If there is breakage between the iterations, the developers know that the previous code worked, so the break must be in the new code. This makes debugging much easier than in the waterfall approach, in which all the code is integrated and tested at the end.

A third benefit of iterative development benefits everyone: The risk of failing to achieve a successful delivery decreases with each iteration. As the project moves forward and the iterations are built, the team is assured of their ability to deliver at least the functionality of the build. In fact, if the crucial functionality is delivered in the early iterations and the "nice-to-haves" in the late iterations, the team can be fully confident that a useful system can be delivered.

The effect of this increasing confidence is that the team's anxiety level decreases as the project proceeds. In contrast, with late integrations in the waterfall process, the team becomes increasingly tense as they approach the test and integration activities, sensing disaster. The integration almost certainly fails at first. How much tear up and rework will be required to fix it is unknown. As the deadline nears, management is likely to panic as well. The team may be called on to exert heroic efforts to save the project. One developer characterized this feeling as akin to being run over slowly by a train.

With a well-run project using the incremental approach, the team has little doubt that the code will come together; that has already been proven. All that is left is to determine how many frills will be included in the delivery. No heroism is required.

5.5 THE RUP PHASES

While the details vary considerably, most software processes have the same set of activities: requirements elicitation and analysis, design, implementation (code, integration), test, and delivery. Most processes also have some iteration scheme. (Even the developers of the waterfall process, notably Winston Royce, promoted iterative waterfalls that consist of several passes through the lifecycle rather than a single pass [Royce, 1998].) The best way to understand and judge a development process is by its phases.

Ideally, process phases meet the human need to mark progress in a project. For psychological and good management reasons, it is important to know how far along you are in the process. Phases answer the question: Are we there yet? In the appendix, I describe a variety of development approaches. Each has a different way of approaching project phases:

- The waterfall approach treats activities as phases. For example, completion of the design marks the end of the design phase.

- The hands-off approach generally ignores phases.

- The rapid prototyping approach treats the iterations as phases.

- In the product development approach, the phases mark the team's joint progress in solving the problem. The development phases are aligned to the problem-solving steps.

Because software development is a collaborative, problem-solving exercise, it makes sense that the software development phases should mark the team's progress toward reaching the solution. This is a key characteristic of the Rational Unified Process.

 Tip Because software development is a collaborative problem-solving exercise, software development phases should mark the team's progress towards reaching the solution.

The Rational Unified Process is illustrated in Figure 5-1, which shows the relationships of three of the main elements of the process: the activities (disciplines and workflows), the phases, and the iterations. As discussed, the phases are directly tied to the activities or the iterations.

Chapter 3 characterized successful software development as an endeavor that solves the following development problem: developing a quality product on a fixed budget and schedule. Rational Unified Process phases—inception, elaboration, construction, transition—are aligned with the stages involved in solving the development problem.

- **Inception:** understanding the development problem. In this phase, the team and stakeholders reach a common understanding of all aspects of the development problem. For some projects, one outcome of the inception phase might be a go/no-go decision. For others, the outcome will be an

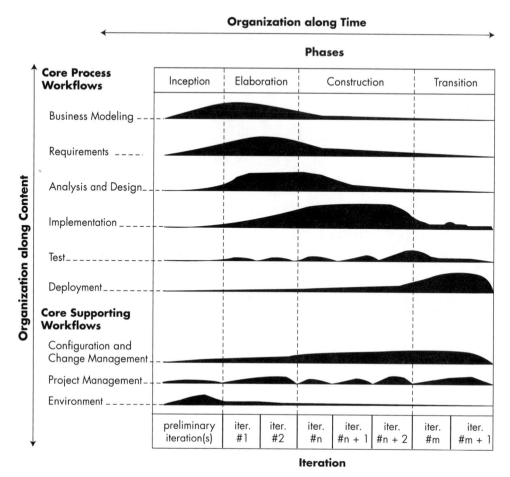

Figure 5-1 The Rational Unified Process

agreement that the project content and boundaries are understood well enough by all stakeholders to permit efficient design.

- **Elaboration:** determining the approach. In this phase, the team determines how it will solve the development problem. During this phase, various approaches to the development might be considered: alternate designs, different choices of technology, and alternative stagings of functionality. Often the outcome is a UML model of the system that is sufficiently detailed to proceed with detailed design and implementation. The architecture has been verified by building an executable code that shows that the software design approach will meet stakeholder needs. An additional outcome is a more detailed project plan for the succeeding phases.

- **Construction:** implementing the approach. In this phase, the approach to the development problem determined during the elaboration phase is carried out. During this phase, the team develops and tests iterations of the software product with each iteration meeting a planned set of use cases. Each iteration enables an increasing set of use cases so that the final iteration is a fully functional, tested version of the code.

- **Transition:** validating the solution. This phase consists of confirming that the software program does in fact meet the stakeholder needs, and it addresses any shortfalls. Testing in this phase is usually in the user's operational setting. This phase ends when the code is ready to be made generally available to the field.

In the Rational Unified Process, a lifecycle is a pass through all four phases. Major milestones indicate the phase transition points, with a milestone marking the end of each phase. Minor milestones occur at the completion of the iterations.

One very important distinguishing characteristic of the Rational Unified Process is that the phases are tied to solving the entire development problem, not just to supplying the code. For example, inception is about the requirements for the larger development problem, not just understanding the requirements for the code. This includes an understanding of the business needs, the market environment, and so on. Throughout the lifecycle, the economic and quality issues are addressed in conjunction with the code development.

The descriptions of the phases are somewhat abstract. They are characterized more by their intent than their activities. The problem for the project manager is to capture the intent of the phases in a project plan, specifying the activities that will be conducted during each phase. This mapping from intent to activities is far from automatic; thought and intellect must be applied. No management template will work for all projects and all organizations. This reality can be a source of frustration for organizations that adopt the Rational Unified Process.

Later sections in this chapter outline the process for developing a project plan, discuss the standard usage model, and describe a standard set of artifacts and outcomes for the elaboration, construction, and transition phases. These discussions are more guidelines than checklists.

5.5.1 The Inception Phase

The following topics are typically addressed during the inception phase:

- Functionality and scope: what will be developed, the scope that will be provided, and other requirements that will be met

- Initial architecture: a high-level design that helps the team and stakeholders to have some notion of the size and effort of the project

- Development plan: agreement on the project milestones, deliverables, schedule, earned value, and staffing

Reaching understanding on all these topics requires a fair amount of analysis. The requirements must be gathered and prioritized, then analyzed sufficiently to determine and confirm the initial architecture. The architecture must be understood well enough that the effort required to carry out the development can be estimated. Finally, all of this information is rolled into the development plan. The inception phase is complete when the team is secure enough about the nature of the project to move on to the elaboration phase.

The inception phase consists of the same activities and outcomes that should be performed and achieved when creating a development proposal or a business case. Some versions of the Rational Unified Process suggest that the outcome of this phase should be a go/no-go decision based on the business case or a funding decision based on a proposal. However, this outcome is appropriate for some projects and is not appropriate for others because the level of information required to make a business or funding decision is less than what is needed to move on to the elaboration phase. For example, the business need might be so evident that there is no time to wait for a completion phase; barring surprises, the project will proceed. Alternatively, perhaps the project proposal was written to be attractive to the reviewers and does not accurately reflect how the development should proceed. In short, a project is often funded even though the development team still has not figured out what they are really going to do. This level of understanding is achieved during the inception phase.

Artifacts developed during the inception phase typically include the use case database, descriptions of the use cases that determine the architecture, and a detailed iteration plan. A good way to end the inception phase is with a formal review with stakeholders. At that review, all acknowledge their common understanding of the project plan and the software to be built.

5.5.2 The Elaboration Phase

This period may be the most difficult yet the most creative for the team. Now that the requirements are fully understood, the team can explore design alternatives and settle on an elegant, logical design. Depending on the nature of the project, deployment considerations may also be addressed during this phase.

Unlike the traditional waterfall approach, a key activity during the RUP elaboration phase is the development of early versions of the code. It is good practice to develop at least one iteration of the system at this time. The purpose of initial iterations is to test out the architecture. Typically, the iterations consist of skeletal versions of the whole system, showing how the components come together (like the chassis of an automobile with mocked-up components). These skeletal versions, sometimes called executable architectures, are an example of applying breadth, then depth. The content of these iterations is chosen to make sure that the technical and development risks are addressed as early as possible.

An 80% complete logical view, discussed in Chapter 2, is a primary product of the elaboration phase. This view should have the breadth to meet all of the expected functionality, but may lack correctness in detail. For that reason the design will change in a limited way throughout the construction phase. With this level of certainty of the design in place, the team is in a position to schedule the iterations of the construction phase. This iteration plan consists of a set of iterations with planned functionality and completion dates. The functionality is described in terms of use cases. Based on this level of detail, the project manager can develop a detailed budget for the completion of the lifecycle.

Like the inception phase, this phase should end with a stakeholder review. All should agree that the design and plan are adequate to solve the development problem.

5.5.3 The Construction Phase

During the construction phase, the team executes the iteration plan developed during the elaboration phase. In practice, the iteration plan is almost never executed without change. Often to hold a schedule, the team will complete an iteration with some planned function missing. Even though this is a setback, as mentioned above, it is fortunate that the slip is immediately evident to the leader. By reviewing the content of the iteration, the leader knows exactly where he or she stands and can decide how to respond.

Doing nothing when functionality is missed in an iteration can result in the *bow wave effect*: The missed function is assigned to a later iteration. That increased function adds more risk to that build, and so it too has missing function. This continues so that more and more function is pushed out to the final build. At that point, it is clear to even the densest manager that the program is behind schedule.

The bow wave is easily avoided. At each iteration, you have to realistically assess the status and develop realistic recovery plans. You have the information to make the adjustments; use it. Sometimes the missing function can be assigned to the next iteration. Sometimes the right answer is to extend the schedule. Sometimes, the right answer is to hold the schedule, but defer some low-priority functionality. This option can be chosen more easily if the iteration plan is constructed with the highest development risk items scheduled as early as possible.

Note that with the greater insight and visibility into the real status of your program, you have the opportunity to uncover and address risk throughout the phase. To be successful, then, you must continually review the status of the iterations, evaluating actual functionality against the plan and then enabling the replanning as needed. In summary, you have better information that you can use to have more control, which in turn can result in a higher likelihood of success. For this to work, you need to make the effort and stay involved.

To end this phase, the code must pass all the system tests: All the use cases targeted for the build are demonstrable.

5.5.4 The Transition Phase

With the completion of the construction phase, the code is built and tested. Just because the code works in the laboratory, however, does not necessarily mean it will work in the field. No matter how carefully you test, there is almost always some set of issues that you do not discover until you put the program into the users' hands.

You have a limited number of machines for system test. Even if the machines are chosen to cover a range of configurations, they may not cover all of the configurations your program may encounter in the field. Your program may not work or may experience some unexpected performance snag on machines that are configured differently than your testing machines.

Another problem is that users are ingenious. Perhaps your team worked closely with the user community, developed use cases, and built the program to support how you expect the users to use the program. The system tests exercised the program, so you have every reason to expect that the users will be satisfied. Most will be. However, you may be delivering the program to thousands or even millions of users. A few of them, perhaps many, will come up with a reasonable, but unexpected, way to use the code. There is no way that your team can anticipate every possible use. This is one reason for beta tests.

Problems can also occur if your system test did not simulate a user environment. For example, some Web-based programs may need to handle tens of thousands of users and tens of millions of data items, and stay up for months at a time. You would like to have some idea how well your program will perform when facing this challenge.

During the transition phase, your team addresses these issues. In this context, transition means moving the code from the laboratory into the users' hands. The transition phase can consist of stress testing, beta testing, and carefully staged installation and switchover at the customer site. You should expect that some amount of code fixing will be necessary. The code fixes should be restricted to those that address operational problems that prevent the customer from using the program in the field. Any function found to be missing is treated as a requirement for a possible later release.

This phase ends when the customer is happily using the product.

5.6 DISCIPLINES AND ARTIFACTS

This section provides an overview of the development disciplines. Each of these activities takes expertise. Numerous books have been written on each of these activities; most of them are longer than this book. Fortunately, you do not need to understand the activities in detail, but you should hire people who do.

The left-hand side of Figure 5-1 shows the disciplines of the Rational Unified Process.

- Business Modeling: developing an understanding of the processes to be supported by the program and determining the best opportunities for automation

- Requirements Management: capturing and maintaining a specification of what the program is supposed to do

- Analysis and Design: modeling the parts of the program, how they are related, and how they meet the requirements

- Implementation: creating the code that meets the design. Implementation includes developing documentation, help files, and training materials.

- Test: verifying that the code meets the requirements

- Deployment: delivering the program to the customer and making sure that it works in the customer's operational environment

Core supporting activities add discipline to the process.

- Configuration Management: maintaining versions of the project artifacts

- Project Management: planning, scheduling, staffing, and tracking the project

- Environment: installing, configuring, and maintaining the project development tools

Each iteration involves some degree of these activities. How much of any given activity is handled in any given iteration depends on how far along you are in the lifecycle. That level is notionally portrayed by the height of the curves in Figure 5-1. (The curve sizes are not meant to be precise.) The results of the activities are captured in the artifacts. Some organizations make up the artifacts project by project; more mature organizations have a company-wide standard set of artifacts.

Only in the past few years, with the adoption of the UML standard, has there been an adequate set of standard artifacts. It is not surprising that many software organizations found it necessary to develop their own artifact formats. Now is a good time to start letting them go. Every organization should consider adopting a UML-based, industry-provided set of artifacts. In this way, every organization can benefit from the intellectual investment of the broader industry. As UML evolves, trying to maintain a competitive advantage without it will be a losing proposition. Whether UML is chosen or not, it is always better to select a standard set of artifacts.

5.6.1 Business Modeling

Some consultants build a business model as a step towards business re-engineering. The model is used to understand what activities the business entities carry out to create value. Business modeling in the Rational Unified Process serves a more modest purpose: It establishes the context in which the program will be used. A piece of software usually supports some user or set of users in carrying out some business process. The software provides the automated support to the user. In order to decide what to automate, it is necessary to understand the business activity that will be supported by the system to be developed. The business model captures this understanding.

The business model also captures who or what will interact with the program (actors, in UML terms) and the enterprise activities that the actors expect to carry out using the program. The activities that the users expect to carry out are captured as business use cases, a textual description of the steps, or IDEF activity models. A business model may also include the objects that are created and maintained as the business proceeds.

For example, if you are building a checking account system for a bank, these might be some of the elements in the business model:

- The actors might include customers, tellers, back office staff members that clear the checks, and other systems (such as ATMs) that interact with the checking account system.

- The use cases might include Making a Deposit, Cashing a Check, and Clearing a Check.

- The objects might include a checking account, a check, and a deposit.

The business model provides input and a framework for determining the detailed requirements. It is maintained as a part of the UML system model.

Some organizations, especially those that build large integrated systems, employ systems engineers. One of their functions is to capture the operational requirements of a system. Often the artifacts created by the systems engineers can fill the need for a business model. These artifacts include functional requirements databases, concept-of-operations documents, context diagrams, and dataflow block diagrams.

5.6.2 Requirements Management

There are two perspectives to requirements management: contractual and collaborative. The traditional view is that requirements form a basis for the contract between the development team and the sponsoring organization. Once the requirements are specified, the program is accepted by "selling off the requirements," that is, testing to prove that each requirement is satisfied. From this point of view, requirements specification enables the stakeholders to know what to expect from the team, and for the developers to prove that they have delivered what was expected.

This contractual approach, as sensible as it sounds, has drawbacks. The goal is to meet the contract, regardless of whether the result is a useful, operational program. Because it is very rare for the requirements to be specified correctly in advance, a program can be delivered that meets specifications but does not meet user needs. As a result, the contracting organization believes that the development group cannot be trusted to meet its promises, and the development group is convinced that contracting organizations can never specify what they want. Everyone loses.

A more modern approach is to treat the specification of requirements as a means of getting all the stakeholders on the same page. Requirements are primarily a way to foster a collaborative relationship between the development team and the people paying for the development so that they can discover together the attributes of a system that would solve the development problem. Rather than one organization laying requirements on the other, both organizations develop their understanding of the requirements and their priorities together. They expect the requirements to change, especially in the details, but they know that is fine as long as the development problem is solved.

This modern understanding of the problem raises a new management challenge: specifying requirements in a way that allows enough change for the right program to get delivered but not so much change that the requirements churn continually. This issue is addressed throughout this chapter.

The three types of requirements maintained in a software program are project vision requirements, functional requirements, and supplemental requirements.

1. The project vision requirements: the high-level description of the project and its purpose. The vision document can be maintained as a text manuscript or as a PowerPoint presentation.

2. Functional requirements: the description of what the program is supposed to do, that is, the services provided to the user.

3. Supplemental requirements: specification of the operational needs of the system, including time limits for providing the various services (performance), how much data needs to be maintained (capacity), and the number of simultaneous users.

We will discuss each of these in turn.

Project Vision   The vision document provides the first step in getting every-one coordinated at the start. Even though the detailed requirements of the project might change, its overall vision should not. The vision document serves as the common reference point for all stakeholders. It provides a view of the project that the developers can buy into as they join the project.

The vision document might contain a description of the business purpose, the intended users, and the proposed features. It is typically developed early in the project, during the inception phase, and is unlikely to change significantly as the project progresses. It must be strategic, not tactical, so it is low on detail. From the breadth-before-depth perspective, the vision document captures the breadth of the system with very little depth. The vision document is useful for communicating the project to executives, customers, and investors.

Creating the document early in the project forces everyone on the project to understand and agree to the big picture before investing too much time in other artifacts. Experience has shown that difficulty in writing a vision document reveals a lack of understanding of the problem. The effort expended in creating the document early prevents missteps later.

Functional Requirements   In UML, the functional requirements are kept as use cases, which are described in Chapter 2. Experience is required to decide exactly how many use cases are sufficient and what their granularity should be (how finely they should be divided). Some analysts try to make every mouse click a use case; others create use cases that cover an entire business operation, such as managing an inventory. The simple rule is that the granularity should be appropriate to reveal the systems architecture. This becomes clearer to the analysts once they have used the use cases as input to the design effort.

Use cases are valuable because they serve as bridging artifacts. They contain enough detail that the users can understand what the system will do and the designers can figure out exactly what needs to be built. As such, they facilitate communications. An additional benefit is that the use case descriptions serve as a suitable starting point for building system test scenarios.

Supplemental Requirements   To make the system useful it is not enough to simply meet the functional requirement. For example, a retail sales sys-tem that takes 30 seconds to scan an item or crashes every 30 minutes is less than useful. The supplemental requirements capture nonfunctional requirements, the operational characteristics the system needs to be useful.

Here are some examples of supplemental requirements:

- System performance: the acceptable amount of time it takes for the system to carry out various tasks

- Capacity: the amount of data the system can store and access without degrading

- Users: the number of simultaneous users allowed

- Availability: the average time between crashes

- Fail over time: the time it takes to bring a crashed system online

Some supplemental requirements, such as performance, can be associated with use cases.

Are We Designing Yet?   Practitioners of the waterfall, serialized, document-driven approach to software development are uncomfortable with creating use case descriptions as part of the requirements specifications task. To them, this seems too much like design. They have been conditioned to believe that design should not begin until the requirements are completely specified. Otherwise, the design effort might be wasted. In this school of thought, requirements are a sequence of "shall" statements, as in "The system shall provide a means for updating checking accounts online." Anything further is thought of as design.

Here is the fallacy: Rigidly separating the listing of requirements from design is not how people approach problems. People need to understand the scope of the problem being solved, to explore their understanding of the problem by thinking through design approaches. One feature that makes use case descriptions effective is that they start the creative process of moving from requirements to design without delving into the system logical architecture.

In practice, development of the logical design and specification of the requirements are overlapping activities, so blending these activities is a good thing.

5.6.3 Analysis and Design

The design activity consists of analyzing the evolving requirements to establish and specify the software architecture. The outcome of this activity is the UML logical, component, and deployment views.

Of all the processes, this is the least mechanical. Converting requirements into designs takes a creative mind that is adept at problem solving. To perform this task well, a person must have a good understanding of the problem and the applicable technologies, as well as design methodologies. This person must be able to apply sound judgment in making design decisions, often with very little information. This person is the system architect. A large project may have more than one system architect: A lead architect takes overall design responsibility; other architects look after their assigned components. The lead architect may have the most important staff role in a project.

The Software Architecture Document   Some features of the architecture are worth documenting and are not captured in the model. Examples of such features include the following high-level considerations:

- The architectural goals and constraints

- The design tradeoffs considered

- The architectural approach adopted

Other topics might include make-versus-buy decisions, and adopted analysis and design patterns. These features of the architecture are not volatile. Because they are unlikely to change throughout the life of the project, they should be contained in a document.

Creating a software architecture document adds to the intellectual property of the organization. It provides a history for case studies and process improvement exercises, including post-mortem meetings. The document also provides a starting place for future architects who need to understand the overall design of the system.

The software architecture document may include a printout of the use case and logical views of the UML model. These views should be maintained in a database, not in a written document. All of the UML modeling tools are databases with special graphical user interface and model display capabilities.

If the UML model must be included in the document for some check-the-box reason mandated by the corporate process, try to change the process. Formatting and printing out the model diminishes the value of the document and adds cost and risk to the project. As a last resort, use the report generation features of the tool to create this content. Be sure to include a disclaimer that only the model is authoritative and the printed document is at best a snapshot in time.

Are We Coding Yet?   Some managers take comfort that the design model includes much of the difficult part of the traditional coding task. One of the 80/20 rules is that 20% of the code does 80% of the work. The 20% includes algorithms, calculations, string and symbol manipulations, and data storage. In object-based languages such as Java and C++, these parts of the code are contained in the code bodies. The remaining 80% of the code consists of declarations such as class specifications, including their methods and attributes. Each method is a function call and so requires a precise list of variables and what kind of data the function returns (the return type). These declarations are the most likely sources of errors in the code because it is difficult to get these details correct in a textual code editor. The design model consists of exactly these details. UML modeling tools generate the 80% of the code that is not contained in the code bodies.

Too often, teams create an analysis model, then abandon the model, and simply start coding, as they did in the 1970s. Modern practice is to evolve the model throughout the development, then use that model to generate the code. Only by following this practice can you be sure that the code is built as designed and designed as built.

Code that is built as designed and designed as built results in an accurate system that is available for maintenance and development of the project.

5.6.4 Implementation

Implementation is the process of creating the code source files that realize the design. A sizable program consists of many source files. Each source code file is a text file that contains the computer instructions expressed in a computer language such as C++ or Java.

The developers create the files and insert the instructions. The individual source files are sometimes called modules. Once a file is ready, it is compiled into machine instructions. This process, performed by a computer, results in another file, sometimes called an object file. The object files are linked with the other object files to make up the executables. A delivered program consists of one or more executables.

It is inevitable that the team will develop more than one version of the code. For many reasons, they must be able to recover previous versions, even after new versions are created. Sometimes an undisciplined programmer introduces a bug into a piece of code that is too hard to find. The best solution is to roll back the code to a known stable version and start the fix over. Sometimes two versions of the code are deliberately created: one to fix a defect, one to add functionality. Eventually, the versions must be merged.

The team must be able to label versions of the code, access them, and reconstruct them. This requirement holds for individual files, collections of files, or the entire system. Fortunately, version control tools allow the team to label the code as a given version and provide mechanisms for branching and merging the source files. They also provide a way to control access to files by providing a checkout, modify, and check-in paradigm. The version control tools support the more formal process of configuration management, which encompasses version control, change request management, and release management.

5.6.5 Test

Planning and executing the testing discipline is remarkably complex. Every project needs a testing strategy that specifies how much the project should invest in what kind of testing. The role of the testing discipline may seem obvious: It is how you verify that the program does what it is supposed to do. This obvious fact hides a variety of issues that should be considered in developing a testing strategy. If these issues are not understood and addressed by your organization, the result can be confusion and unnecessary conflict.

Problems may arise because different stakeholders have different perspectives on what it means to get a working program. For example, the developers might be concerned that the program works as intended; the users might be concerned that the program performs the functions they need; the architects are concerned that the program is built as designed. The integration and test group may want to be sure that the program works well with others, that it does not hog resources or slow down the system.

Different kinds of testing deal with each of these issues.

- Unit tests confirm that each of the individual modules does what the developers expect.

- Component tests confirm that each of the components or subsystems behaves as the architects expect.

- System functional tests confirm that the system behaves as the users expect.

- System operational tests confirm that the system functions well in an operational environment, that it works as the integration and test group expects.

Testing is expensive, and research has shown that it produces diminishing returns. As the defect density (the number of defects per line of code) decreases, the amount of testing it takes to uncover the next bug increases exponentially. Once most of the defects have been found, it can take 40 (or 200) hours of testing to find the next defect. Finding the last few defects in good code is very expensive.

Two affordable approaches enable you to get enough testing time on the systems to be confident that many of the defects are discovered:

- Automated testing: Automated test tools simulate customer interactions and large customer loads.

- Beta testing: Your customers do the testing for free.

Either approach requires an investment, but given the number of hours it takes to uncover defects, the investment is justified. The alternative could be marshaling hundreds of testers working three shifts a day, seven days a week. Beta testing is especially attractive because the beta testers provide their own environments, enabling you to exercise the code in a larger number of settings than you can afford to put into a laboratory. Microsoft implements extensive beta programs before every product launch.

Are We Done Yet?   You will inevitably be faced with deciding when the program is good enough to ship. The answer is not "when all of the bugs are gone." It is impossible to find the last bug for programs of any size and complexity: The cost may be prohibitive, and you never know if you have found the last bug. Ultimately, every manager must make an economic decision: Is it more cost-effective to ship the code than to wait and continue testing?

Waiting adds development expense and adds risk that you might not meet the market opportunity, lowering revenue. Shipping too soon can be a customer relations nightmare and lead to unacceptable service costs. In the worst case, you may lose credibility with your customers and go out of business. Achieving the right balance depends on your situation. The criteria are different for video games and Space Shuttle navigation systems.

Most organizations classify defects in four categories:

1. Must-fix defects: These cause the code to be unusable or, even worse, to corrupt the customer's system or data. Code that crashes or freezes frequently has must-fix defects.

2. Should-fix defects: These cause the code to be less useful than the customer expects. For example, one of the functions does not work properly, or performance of some functions is unacceptable.

3. Nice-to-fix defects: These cause the code to be less satisfactory or efficient than it would be if the defect were removed. Examples include user interface changes and minor performance improvements.

4. Deferrable defects: These may be desired enhancements reported as defects. Deferrable defects may also be the result of a tester performing a very improbable sequence of interactions. For example, the tester holds down the Esc key, hits the F7 key 25 times as fast as possible, and the system freezes. The solution is not to perform this activity.

Track the discovery rate (defects per hour of testing) during beta testing and automated testing. If the discovery of new defects is dwindling to zero and there are no known type 1 or 2 defects, you are probably ready to ship. This is always a judgment call.

Testing versus Quality Assurance   The role of testing in delivering a quality system is often misunderstood. Think of the code as a beautifully designed chair. As you build the chair, you make sure the materials meet the specification, and that each piece of the chair meets the specification. You sand carefully as you go. Once the chair is assembled, you measure to be certain it meets the specification. You sit in the chair to test whether it is as comfortable as you intended. You move it around to be sure it holds its shape. In response to these tests, you may make some small adjustments; you do not redesign the chair. The quality is in the design, the choice of materials, and the workmanship. The testing ensured that the quality inherent in the design was delivered.

You cannot test quality; this is a development truism. Testing and defect removal are used to polish up the code so that you can deliver the quality inherent in the design. Quality must be addressed throughout the development cycle.

You cannot test quality. Testing and defect removal polish up the code so that you can deliver the quality inherent in the design.

Defects are easy to find and remove in well-designed code. Fixing a bug does not result in a new bug; the removal of a defect does not result in a redesign. If your experience is different—if each fix introduces a new bug or the fixes result in significant design changes—you have design problems. In this case, it is unlikely that any number of test-and-fix cycles will result in a quality delivery. In fact, you may never be able to ship! If you suspect your code is in this state, call a time-out and work with the technical leads to review the adequacy of the current design, planning to fall back to the elaboration phase.

5.6.6 Deployment

Deployment means delivering the code to the user. It may include packaging the code for general sale or installing the code at the customer site. Deployment activities often include creating installation procedures and distribution media such as CD-ROMs. These activities are straightforward but must be planned and budgeted.

5.7 PROJECT MANAGEMENT

All projects require these project management functions:

- Establishing a detailed plan that includes deliverables, a schedule of events and activities, a work breakdown structure, and a staff loading plan

- Acquiring the resources required to carry out the plan

- Tracking the progress of the project against the plan

- Cajoling the staff to stick to the plan

- Communicating the status of the project to management

An underlying assumption of classical project management is that enough information exists to create a detailed plan that is likely to be followed. From there on, it is only necessary to work to the plan. As discussed in Chapter 3, there is not enough firm information with software development projects to create a detailed plan. This lack of information is a great source of frustration for all concerned.

As the project progresses, the understanding of the requirements, the design, and the associated effort improves, enabling improved detail planning. To cope, the software project manager needs a way to specify the plan at various levels of detail. The highest level of the plan has major milestones and not much else. It may be shared with management and the customer. At the detailed level, with iteration boundaries, the plan must be flexible enough to accommodate new information that is important to the developers. It may or may not be shared with the customer.

The Rational Unified Process provides these mechanisms. Although the project plan calls for a set number of iterations for each phase, the content of the iterations is only roughly specified. For example, the plan may call for half of the classes to be implemented by the second iteration in the construction phase; it does not specify which classes. During the construction phase, the project manager, in consultation with the team leads, determines which classes will be implemented. The ability to adjust the order of development allows the project management to manage internal dependencies and adjust for unexpected problems that always arise during development. Because this level of detail is not surfaced in the plan, it is possible to hold to the plan while making the necessary adjustments.

The necessity of paying attention to the detailed activities and adjusting the detailed plan should not be taken as a mandate to micromanage the work. It should provide an opportunity to facilitate the work of the developers. By adjusting the content, you can help the developers stay productive.

5.8 THE WORST THING YOU CAN DO

Above all, it is important not to abandon the process in times of perceived crises. One sure path to the next crisis is to decide, when the schedule or budget is tight and the delivery is crucial, that all the process is getting in the way and the team should concentrate solely on delivering the code. In almost every case, the outcome will be a disaster. The delivery will not be met and the damage to the organization will be considerable. You will have conveyed to the team that all of the investment made in providing an effective process was a luxury.

In a crunch, the answer is not to drop the process but to accelerate it. Go through all the phases; do the iterations; just do them faster. You can consider ways to limit the size of the project by abbreviating some of the artifacts, but otherwise, hold to the process.

5.9 THE REWARD: IMPROVED RESULTS

At first, managers often find the Rational Unified Process to be unsettling. Although many standard project management techniques apply, many do not.

The Rational Unified Process is sufficiently different in its planning, implementation, and oversight that it requires new management skills and behavior.

The flexibility inherent in the Rational Unified Process requires the project manager to pay constant attention to team activities and to understand those activities in detail so that appropriate adjustments can be made. This may take more time and energy than anticipated in planning the project management activities. Walker Royce points out that the management effort doubles from 5% to 10% of the overall effort when this approach is adopted [Royce, 1998]. However, the investment is rewarded by a superior outcome.

In particular, the Rational Unified Process takes more management effort than the waterfall process; there are more control and decision points. These control points provide the skilled software development manager with more opportunities to manage the development risks facing the project, enhancing the probability of a successful outcome. With the Rational Unified Process, managers at all levels are more involved with the project. This is a good thing. Constructive management involvement typically indicates an effective software organization. The Rational Unified Process provides a framework for this involvement.

Adopting the Rational Unified Process facilitates the development but makes its management more challenging. The increased management effort results in a more successful outcome.

TO LEARN MORE

The definitive text on the Rational Unified Process is

- Kruchten, Philippe. *The Rational Unified Process, An Introduction* (2nd ed.), Addison-Wesley, 2000.

The three founders of UML provide their perspective in the following text. It contains more details of the activities and artifacts in a UML context.

- Jacobson, Ivar, Grady Booch, and James Rumbaugh. *The Unified Software Development Process*, Addison-Wesley, 1999.

Royce's text expands on his economics model found in Chapter 4 to draw lessons on managing software projects. His discussion of the top ten principles of software development is particularly insightful.

- Royce, Walker. *Software Project Management: A Unified Framework*, Addison-Wesley, 1998.

My previous text goes through the RUP process phase-by-phase providing practical information about managing a project adopting the process.

- Cantor, Murray. *Object-Oriented Project Management with UML*, John Wiley, 1998.

The following series provides some useful insights and advice in applying the process.

- Ambler, Scott and Larry Constantine. *The Unified Process Construction Phase: Best Practices in Implementing the UP*, CMP Books, 2000a.

- Ambler, Scott and Larry Constantine. *The Unified Process Inception Phase: Best Practices in Implementing the UP*, CMP Books, 2000b.

- Ambler, Scott, Larry Constantine, and Roger Smith. *The Unified Process Elaboration Phase: Best Practices in Implementing the UP*, CMP Books, 2000.

Finally, one of the earliest and best books describing the benefits of iterative development is the following:

- Booch, Grady. *Object Solutions: Managing the Object-Oriented Project*, Addison-Wesley, 1996.

Chapter 6

Management and Leadership

This final chapter gives guidance to all, but especially to managers, on how to provide leadership to software organizations. In particular, it explains how to achieve the right level of involvement to keep the projects on track while enabling the necessary communication for the team to be successful.

As discussed in earlier chapters, successful software projects are characterized by the following characteristics:

- A problem-solving paradigm

- Iterative development of all artifacts, including the project plan

- Diseconomy of scale (more people can slow down the work)

- Inherent unpredictability

Leading projects with these special attributes takes special skills; those skills are the topic of this chapter.

A recent television commercial for IBM shows a senior manager and her staff around a table discussing how to solve a crisis. The corporate Web server has crashed, and she is trying to lay blame. In response to her impatient questions, her staff tells her that the server people blame the database people, who in turn blame the application people. Her staff looks more disgusted than guilty. Clearly angry, she asks, "Whose job is it to see that all of this stuff works together?" Someone whispers in her ear, "That would be your job," leaving her stunned and silent.

This 30-second drama is full of lessons for the development leader.

- This manager had no view of the technology under her stewardship. She did not understand it well enough to staff properly, let alone provide oversight. An important role, the system integrator, was left unfilled. She knew enough to assign some of the responsibilities, but not enough to cover all the bases.

- The manager did not have any mechanism for assessing the health and status of the technology. It broke without warning, and she had no basis for remedial action.

- Whether or not she trusted her people, she had neither their trust nor respect.

- In the end, her authority and bullying failed her. She may have been the manager, but she was not a leader. She needed to have an involved, collaborative relationship with her staff.

6.1 LEADERSHIP STYLE

Consider the following example. Your job is to plan the work and lead the effort to create a 10,000-page document in six months. You know that no one person can accomplish this task, that you will need a team of people for the project. Your research shows that a competent writer can create a polished draft, edited and revised, at the rate of about six pages per day. Using 20 working days per month, a back-of-the-envelope calculation shows that you need 14 writers.

Once you bring the writers on board, how do you proceed? You can explain the project at a team meeting and send the writers to their cubicles to begin working. Although this seems foolish, some managers approach software development this way. In the example at hand, you would find that the writers try to perform. They soon find that most of their time is spent trying to coordinate their efforts: who is going to write what. Productivity falls far below six pages a day. Even so, the last thing you want is to add another writer, which would only exacerbate the problem.

Another approach to the project would be to dole out the chapters one by one to the writers, keeping the big picture to yourself. As chapters are turned in, you see inconsistencies among them. At first this is not a problem; you function as the editor, marking up each chapter and directing changes that iron out the differences. This process becomes more and more time consuming as you edit the revisions. You become a bottleneck for the entire project. Your staff sits idle while you plow through the document again, trying to achieve consistency. You are frazzled, the document gets delivered late, and you realize that you wrote the entire book.

A better approach would be for the manager to assign a head writer to create an outline for the document, divide the writers into teams, and assign one or more chapters to each team, grouping chapters by similarity of content. The manager would also hire people to review, assess, and edit the teams' output, working with the head writer. The head writer would answer questions concerning which content would be where, arbitrate disputes, and create a style guide. If the document needs to be changed, the head writer would work with the chapter teams to reassign content. The manager would periodically review progress against plan and constructively address any problems uncovered. The manager would also work to head off requests for unnecessary changes. The manager stays involved, creates and monitors the structure that facilitates the work, and does whatever is necessary to keep the work on track.

As in the example, most development managers exhibit one of three leadership styles: uninvolved, in complete control, or a member of the team.

1. The Uninvolved Manager In the extreme, uninvolved middle and senior managers determine the business need, assign a schedule and budget, and assign project managers to connect the dots. They take no further role in the project except for ad hoc review meetings. Because they have not provided for the inevitable changes in scope and design, their projects rarely go according to plan. The project managers may be saddled with plans they do not believe in. When things inevitably go wrong, upper management blames the staff. These managers are prone to complaining about the incompetence of most programmers. Sometimes they initiate process improvements, ordering their staff to improve productivity and the like. Under these circumstances, the looked-for improvement rarely occurs. Eventually, the managers lose interest, unaware that they might be part of the problem.

Hackers are the usual reason software ever gets written in teams with uninvolved managers. *Hackers* are special people who are very productive programmers. Uninvolved managers rely on these hackers, who may do 80 percent of the work. The rest of the staff merely assists the hackers. Uninvolved managers think their job is to hire the best people they can, hoping to land a hacker or two. Once the hackers are on board, the managers talk them into building the necessary applications, give them what they need, and let them work their magic. With any luck, they are rewarded with working code and not excuses. Hackers often have their own ideas and deliver innovative code that does meet the stakeholders' needs.

This is no way to run a business. Each project is an adventure, with no two projects alike. The manager is at the mercy of the hackers: They may deliver; they may not. There is no way to know. The manager has no basis for knowing whether schedules are reasonable. Even worse, hackers who walk out may take all understanding of the program with them.

This is also no way to live. Management oversight consists of continually asking the developers whether they are finished, expressing disappointment at any lack of progress, and suggesting that the team works harder. The relationship may become adversarial, with the manager reduced to berating the staff and the staff treating the manager with disdain. The manager's job may be on the line, with no control over keeping promises to upper management. This is a perfect recipe for stress.

2. The In Complete Control Manager   Managers who strive for complete control treat their staff as appendages. These managers, often promoted from the technical ranks, trust no one but themselves and insist that all communications flow through them. Any communications between a pair of developers are inconsequential. Imagine a wheel with the manager at the center and developers on the rim, with communications restricted to flowing through the spokes. The leader makes all the decisions and the staff can only carry out his or her will. These managers are always on their own critical path, which is an untenable and stressful position.

As the project grows, the communications channels become increasingly inefficient. The manager becomes the bottleneck. On a project that is even moderate in size, team members will eventually need to communicate among themselves. Other channels spontaneously emerge as they try to fill in the gaps, carrying out roles beyond their assignments. This happens without the manager's knowledge. By attempting to maintain complete control, the manger will ultimately lose influence over the project.

3. The Team Member Manager   Managers who function as team members understand that they must be involved with, but not at the center of, their projects. They understand their role on the team and know how to participate as the leader while trusting and empowering their staff. I am sure it comes as no surprise that I recommend this approach.

6.2 TEAM LEADERSHIP

To be effective, a manager must take a leadership role on the team. This is different from a technical leadership role, but just as crucial. The role consists of looking after several key management elements:

- The team framework: putting in place the appropriate roles, staff assignments, tools, and processes

- The big picture: seeing that the effort continues to meet the business need, that it has the correct content, schedule, and budget

- Team dynamics: making sure the project team and individuals are communicating effectively

Most managers will do the first task, fret about the second, and pretty much ignore the third. These tasks cannot be carried out unless the manager is continually involved with the project. The challenge is to find a constructive way to stay involved without being the project bottleneck. The key point is that the role of manager is one of the various team roles. However, it is special in a few ways:

- The manager looks after the project as a whole, the large-scale structure of the effort. It follows that the manager cannot be involved with the details; detail work must be assigned to developers.

- The manager treats the project as a dynamic system, using influence to provide the necessary steering.

6.2.1 Being the Manager

"Manager" is one of the development project roles. It is useful to consider this role as simply one of the various roles on the project, and the manager as one of the team, one of the entities interacting with all the others so that the team can carry out the project. The manager does not oversee or supervise from the outside; the manager is on the inside.

As the leader, the manager must be the most aware of the team dynamics and the effectiveness of the organization. In particular, the manager must continually steer the team to make sure that communications are sufficient and the team as a whole is working toward the right goals. Managers must work at the broadest scope, avoiding involvement in the details.

As you approach the manager's role, remember that continual steering is necessary. No amount of upfront planning will guarantee a predicted outcome for a software project. Projects cannot be expected to stay on track without guidance. Like an automobile on the field, projects are continually buffeted by external forces such as changing requirements, unexpected difficulties with components, friction among staff members, and so on. There is one thing you can be sure of: The project will not go according to any detailed plan you develop at the outset. Although constant oversight is necessary to keep the project on track, rigorous control is not required. A light touch is all that is needed. Review the status and the short-term, detailed plans to make sure they are consistent with the project goals. Usually it is sufficient to ask searching questions and expect crisp answers.

Managers like detailed plans because they seem to provide a mechanism for establishing and maintaining control. However, projects involve luck, uninformed estimates, and the complications of team interactions, so project plans are at best good guesses as to how the work will evolve. No amount of detail will change this ambiguity. In fact, the more detailed the initial plan, the more likely it will not be followed. It is best to create a high-level plan and continually work the details as the project evolves.

There is tension between these points. You need to steer, but not control. Managing a project may be more like riding a horse than driving a car. The best riders form a team with a horse, relying on its skills and judgment. Hold the reins, but not too tightly.

Applying these lessons takes trust and faith, along with an understanding of team dynamics. To quote Margaret Wheatley, one of the founders of the application of chaos theory to management practice, "Do not play God, trust the universe, and play a role" [Wheatley, 1999].

6.2.2 Organizing to Enable Communications

The manager's first opportunity to facilitate an orderly project comes with assigning roles and responsibilities. Various mechanisms exist for establishing formal communications channels. The most obvious approach is to create development teams using a hierarchical organization chart. In the old paradigm, organization charts were about lines of control; in the new paradigm, they are more about responsibility.

The best use of organization charts is to define roles, centers of ownership, and responsibility. They provide a way for the manager to communicate who is responsible for what to the team. Responsibility flows downward so that people high in the chart take some responsibility, technical or managerial, for the work of the people below them. The organization chart provides a mechanism for making sure the work is covered.

Members of a development team communicate frequently with each other but rarely with members of other development teams. The manager can take advantage of this phenomenon by portioning out work to different teams in logical subsystems. Because developers working on the same subsystem need to work together closely, they should be on the same team.

Some managers believe that communications should flow up and down the hierarchy established in the organization chart. They believe that development team members who cross team boundaries may come to agreements without involving their leadership, reaching decisions that are not properly reviewed and that put the integrity of the project at risk. This belief, if enforced, leads to equilibrium, with all of its disadvantages.

Effective communications are an extension of the organization chart. The project team must be allowed and encouraged to find the communications channels they need; they will anyway. Managers can promote communications by establishing cross-functional teams that reinforce the need to communicate. For example, you might create a design team consisting of the lead architect and the design leads from each of the subsystem teams.

Architecture-Based Project Organization   The architecture is the structure of the program and a key artifact, as discussed in Chapter 2. The logical decomposition partitions the program into functional blocks that collaborate to provide the overall code functionality. The code within the subsystems is tightly coupled, and the subsystems communicate with defined interfaces. The people working on the subsystems must have frequent communications to coordinate and agree on these interfaces.

It is interesting to observe how well you can match the code and the team communications models. Creating a project organization like the one shown in Figure 6-1 and assigning logical subsystems to various development teams fosters a close-to-optimal communications model. The subsystem architecture leads can work with the system architecture to work out the large design. Work on the details can be contained within the subsystem teams. Modern design tools also provide mechanisms that support the communications model. These tools allow the model to be partitioned so that some people can work on details of part of the design while technical leaders can be sure that the overall integrity is preserved.

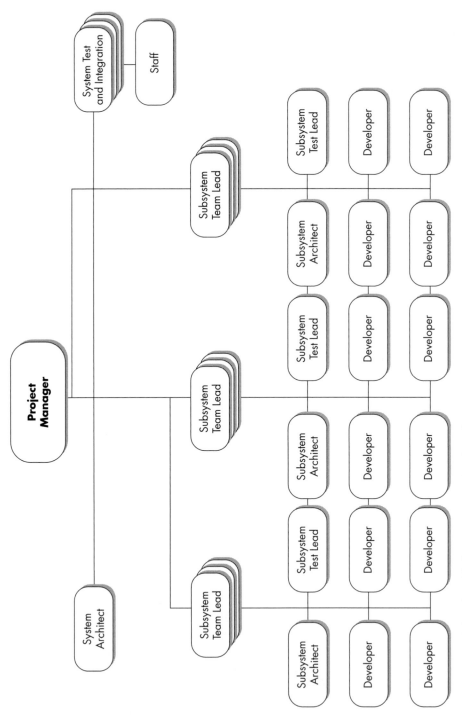

Figure 6-1 Rational Unified Process Organization Chart

The design tools also identify which parts of the code interact. These code interactions provide the basis for cross-team discussions.

6.2.3 Constructive Involvement

A fundamental implication of the new common sense is that managers must find a way to relinquish control and be constructively involved with the projects. A non-linear system needs gentle steering to proceed to a predicted outcome. However, overly controlled systems lack the ability to reset the connections, the communications paths, or to adapt to a changing environment.

In the long run, an orderly project does not result from control. Paradoxically, when managers insist on being in control, they prevent real order from emerging. Roles tend to be narrow and overdefined. Quality team members who are committed to the project's success or whose egos are bruised by the lack of implied trust resist being overmanaged and work around the system. When they find the roles and communications paths restrictive and inadequate, they invent their own. These creative solutions may be invisible to management and may not be optimal in terms of project goals. Chaos can result. This is the insight behind satires such as *Catch 22*.

Realistically, if a project is considerably off base, a manager may need to take full control to bring it back on track. This action is often necessary when the manager has been uninvolved up to that point. Setting short-term goals of a few weeks' duration and directing team members' efforts in meeting those goals usually produce good results. The manager should make sure that team members understand the necessity for this process. During this time, communications with team members should be increased, and roles and communications paths should be reset so that control can be safely relinquished.

The Rational Unified Process provides the mechanisms for the manager to be constructively involved:

- The iterations, with demonstrable progress, provide a way to steer the project and to manage success.

- The phases provide a method for acknowledging and reinforcing common levels of understanding.

These features provide the leader the means to steer the project without paralyzing it. As the project moves from phase to phase, be sure you understand how the solution to the development problem has evolved. Review the iterations; be aware of what the iteration contained and what was planned. Participate in the iteration plan and its adjustments. Share in the content management; decide with the team whether content needs to be deferred to hold the schedule.

Project Reviews   Project reviews provide the manager with an accurate status of the current health, status, and stability of the project. The review should be scheduled frequently with a consistent format. Properly handled, reviews provide a forum where team members can bring up problems or the manager can uncover problems while there is still time to react constructively.

Reviews typically include the following topics:

- Overall project status, including risks and mitigations. The staff briefs management on how the project is doing, what problems are emerging, and what help is needed. Figure 6-2 shows a suitable format for presenting this information.

- Artifact status. The review should include status and activity of project artifacts such as architecture documents, vision plans, and test plans. In the Rational Unified Process, each artifact should be at a specified level of completion as the phases are completed. However, the artifacts are under

Risk	Status	Cause	Mitigation
Schedule (likelihood the current schedule will be met)	Green: little risk; no action needed. Yellow: some risk; action required. Red: serious risk; urgent action required.	Root cause of the problem such as missed dependencies, skill shortfalls, or slow staffing	Planned, ongoing mitigation, status
Budget (likelihood the current budget will be met)	Green: little risk; no action needed. Yellow: some risk; action required. Red: serious risk; urgent action required.	Root cause of the problem, such as changed requirements	Planned, ongoing mitigation, status
Customer Satisfaction (likelihood the content will be acceptable)	Green: little risk; no action needed. Yellow: some risk; action required. Red: serious risk; urgent action required.	Root cause of the problem, such as customer needs changing or inadequate customer feedback	Planned, ongoing mitigation, status

Figure 6-2 Risk Summary

constant revision and should be addressed, if only in passing, at every review.

- Overall schedule status and stability. Changes in the schedule baseline at the macro or micro levels should be presented, as well as any slips against the current schedule, their cause, and mitigation plan.

- Iteration plan status. The iteration plan is especially dynamic and should be the source of ongoing discussion. The content of the previous iteration and the planned content of the current iteration should be presented. Any slipped content should be noted, and the iteration that will include the missing content should be discussed.

- Financial status. Standard cost and schedule variances with associated ratios are used to track whether spending is as planned for the amount of work accomplished as of a given time. These metrics can be applied by determining the *earned value,* a measure of the value of the work accomplished to date. This is best done by assigning a value to the artifacts and to the content in the iterations. For example, each use case planned for an iteration will have an earned value that can be claimed only when testing is successfully completed.

- Progress and stability metrics. For each key artifact such as use cases and class objects, a set of metrics that shows the stability of the current number to be included in the build and the completion against plan is reviewed. Figure 6-3 shows one way to track progress and stability. *Original scope* is the number of artifacts planned when the schedule was created; *current scope* is the number of artifacts currently planned to be delivered; *current planned* is the number of artifacts that were planned to be completed by the date in the chart; *current implemented* is the number actually implemented. If current scope is different than original scope, the project is unstable and there is reason for concern. If currently implemented differs from the plan, this also indicates a problem.

- Action item status. This standard list of action items from previous reviews indicates whether the action item is open or closed and gives other relevant information.

The reviews should involve minimal preparation and should not add cost or risk to the project. Once the project is up and running, an hour of preparation

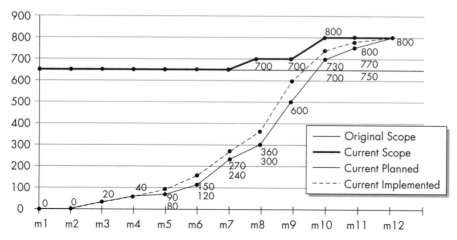

Figure 6-3 Progress and Stability Graph

should be adequate. Ideally, metrics and financial data would be collected through automated tracking and reporting tools. The reviews should be short, focused, and disciplined. They should be scheduled for and completed in one hour. Any issues that need more time should be noted and addressed in a separate session. Team members will appreciate the discipline and the implied respect for their time.

It is critical that managers react constructively to the information gained in reviews, looking for ways to help, not criticize. If there is instability or slippage, the manager may be able to help by going to the source, locating an essential resource, or negotiating with a fellow manager. The manager may help resolve customer communications issues or even to bring the program to baseline again, if necessary. This is an opportunity for the manager to build trust and reinforce project roles.

At project reviews, accuracy, not precision, is important. All of the measures and metrics presented indicate the actual status of the project. They should be the most accurate reflection possible of everyone's understanding of the program because they will be used as a basis for action. At best, however, measures and metrics can only approximate the complexity of a real project. They are likely to be imprecise and will gain in precision as the project evolves. For example, it is well known that the cost-to-complete for most projects is very imprecise in the early stages. Precision is gained as the development problem is understood. Holding the staff to a precise estimate early is unreasonable and shows that the manager is not part of the team. On the other hand, tracking this value is worthwhile because it indicates progress. If the cost-to-complete settles to a value consistent with the time remaining and remains stable, it indicates that the needed level of understanding of the project has been achieved. This also applies to the other variables.

Maintaining the Vision   Some say that leading developers is like herding cats. Each cat has its own goal, not shared by the group, and pursues it. By comparison, a hunting pack of wolves is very orderly, focused on the goal of finding prey. As a manager, you want your team to perform like the wolves, not the cats. For this to happen, the team must have the same "prey" in mind. You must clearly delineate the business and technical goals of the project. The team must understand what it means to be successful, what the business priorities are, and why the project matters to the organization. They need to feel that belonging to a successful team will reflect well on them individually and management will appreciate them.

It is important to decide how much information to share with the team. Some managers believe that the developers need to know only the requirements and the schedule. The team goal is to meet the requirements on the dates specified. Although this limited view may suffice for simple projects, it is often too constraining and leads to failure. Unless the team is confident that the requirements are sufficient and correct and that the allotted time is reasonable, they will believe that no real goal has been set. They will waste time fretting over what they should be doing while the project becomes increasingly chaotic.

Recently, I was consulting with one of the world's largest automobile manufacturing firms, a company known for the quality of their cars. This firm was not equally proficient at developing in-house systems for running the business. In fact, this development group consistently failed to deliver on commitments. I was asked to provide a seminar to a development team on project planning.

I started with a discussion of coming to a shared vision on the business goals of the project and a commotion broke out. One of the managers in attendance took me aside and explained emotionally that this sort of information was never shared with the development staff. I asked how the team knew how to make trades between functionality and time-to-field. The manager said that the business analysts had met with the users and management and had provided all that was needed in the requirements. Anyhow, what was really needed, the manager told me, was a project plan that some other customer had used successfully. They would just copy it. This was the manager of a team that had failed for six months to make any headway understanding the requirements.

In this culture, managers only worried about control and stayed aloof from the projects. They were looking for the magic project plan that would guarantee success. I regret that after much discussion over several months, the managers never did change behavior and the organization is still failing to deliver.

The moral is that sharing the broader business needs enables team members to find a path toward success. The manager then has the flexibility to provide a plan that accounts for refining and prioritizing the requirements and setting the development effort.

Being a Filter   Management itself is often the source of chaos. It is common for managers who are sensitive to customer or market needs to order frequent changes in priorities and vision. This is like telling the wolf pack every half-hour to change the prey they are stalking from deer to antelope to raccoon. The hunt would probably fail and all would go hungry. Experienced middle managers and project leads realize that they must protect their teams and projects from high-frequency inputs from the top. They become filters in the communications channel from upper management to their teams. They eliminate high-frequency noise so that a low-frequency, slowly changing message is delivered.

The team may have heard that an upper manager wants a change in product content. To squelch rumors, the project lead might tell the team that even though management wants a feature added to the software, there are no changes in the plans for the current effort, and the feature may be included in the future.

Sometimes change is needed and the vision must be reset, such as when an unexpected competitive product enters the market. The management team should share the need for change with the team, explaining why it is important that the project plan and development efforts be adjusted and clearly expressing the new vision. It is important for management to be sensitive to the stress caused by the change, expressing appreciation for the difficulty it will cause.

Avoid Slogans   After completion of the Space Shuttle, NASA managers, faced with budget cuts, began looking for ways to accomplish their mission with fewer funds. They realized that some of their programs could go forward using less expensive designs. For example, when the Mars rover landed on Mars in an inflated tetrahedron, the rover could deploy regardless of which face of the tetra-hedron ended up on the surface. This discovery led to a cheaper and better design. Wanting to encourage this sort of creative thinking, management adopted the slogan "Faster, Better, Cheaper."

Unfortunately, the success of the Mars rover was followed by a series of failures, including the highly publicized crash of the Mars Climate Orbiter. The failure was caused by a failure of communications between project teams: One team used metric units; the other used inches. Both teams' modules worked as designed, but the system failed.

According to a recent report [NASA, 2000], the failure was traced to several failures in management, especially blind adherence to the slogan. In the "Faster, Better, Cheaper" culture, NASA managers were expected to find the optimal balance of scope and cost so that the risk profile was flat. I am not sure how this can be done; apparently, neither was NASA management. The report states: "As implementation of the (Faster, Better, Cheaper) strategy evolved, however, the focus on cost and schedule reduction increased risk beyond acceptable levels on some NASA projects." This outcome is hardly surprising. Analysis of the software economics model discussed in Chapter 4 shows that the project manager trades off cost, schedule, and risk. For example, for a project to be faster, either the team skips steps, which adds quality risk, or adds staff, which increases cost.

The NASA report suggests a new slogan, "Mission First." Most of the recommendations for implementing the slogan are consistent with the messages in this book. Hopefully, they will focus on improved leadership and not the slogan.

This NASA experience illustrates the dangers of what Tom Demarco and Timothy Lister call "management by slogan" [Demarco and Lister, 1999]. Management develops a vision of how their staff should act, and then captures the vision in a slogan, printing posters and holding all-hands meetings to roll out the campaign. Usually, the slogan is not accompanied by changes in the behavior of senior managers. If the slogan is accompanied by changes in oversight, budgeting, and staffing procedures, there is hope for the initiative. Without such changes, this approach is merely a variation on the uninvolved management approach. The hidden message is that management is okay, but the staff needs to change.

Unless the initiative is well founded, with a phased adoption or transition plan, it is likely to appear naïve and silly. It may reinforce the staff's impression that management is out of touch and has little to contribute that is constructive. Ultimately, the exercise may create a distance between management and the team that diminishes management's ability to stay involved and provide the oversight and steering called for in the new paradigm.

Managing Success   Walker Royce often points out that success management, rather than risk management, is critical to effective leadership. A standard maxim of personnel management is that individuals, once their basic needs for food and shelter are met, are motivated by personal growth and the quality of their work. It is not surprising then that people prefer to work on successful projects. If the team perceives their efforts to be successful and appreciated, they are more likely to perform well.

One approach to taking advantage of this phenomenon is to manage a project as a series of successes, starting with small successes and building to larger ones. The Rational Unified Process iterations provide a mechanism for this series of successes. Each of the early project iterations projects should be carefully crafted so that as the iterations come together, (1) they will be successful, and (2) project risks are addressed. With the completion of the iteration, the team feels successful and becomes increasingly confident that they will deliver. This confidence is self-reinforcing and the team becomes increasingly motivated.

As obvious as this may seem, many managers fail to capitalize on this effect. Rather than promoting success, they emphasize the fear of failure. Perhaps motivated by fear, they are afraid to give praise, believing that the team will become complacent and start slacking off. With each success, they take care to lecture at their team. They may say something like, "That was pretty good, but this is no time to slack off." Failure to appreciate a team's progress and success can lead to a sort of despair; team members may adopt a "What's the use?" attitude and stop trying.

6.2.4 Working with Developers

Computers are marvelous in their complexity. The average home computer executes hundreds of millions of operations per second: retrieving values from memory, carrying out arithmetic operations, storing intermediate values, saving data to disk, updating the screen, sending data to the printer, and so on, while servicing input from the keyboard and the mouse. The actual state of the computer—the values stored in its memory and its various special registers—also changes hundreds of millions of times a second. Yet one flaw (a bug) in one value at any given moment can be catastrophic; the system may crash or, more insidiously, the wrong data may be generated or stored. Users expect programs to run for hours, days, even months, without one of these bugs appearing.

It is the programmer's job to generate instructions so that the computer does the work intended without any bugs. It is easy to see why this is difficult. The programs generated these days often have millions of lines of instructions, any one of which may contain a subtle error. But that's not the worst of it. Often the order in which the instructions are executed depends on the user; one set of mouse clicks creates a different execution path than another. Since today's computers are designed to run several programs at the same time, the way a given program executes often depends on which other programs are also running on the system. Therefore, the programmer cannot be sure exactly how a program will run in the field.

Tip

A software program is a complex system that may contain millions of instructions executed in some unpredictable order at hundreds of millions of operations per second. Often programs must run flawlessly for days at a time. The resulting program must meet customer and market needs.

Given this complexity, it's amazing that people can develop software at all. How did humans evolve the capability to control an unrelentingly logical machine? The needed skills have little to do with hunting, evading prey, or attracting a mate. Nevertheless, we have arrived at a point where software is central to our economic and cultural life and programmers are able to write that software.

The fact that programmers can control the unforgiving machine makes them different and creates a sense of separation from those who cannot. It is hard to describe the sense of power and satisfaction that results from having the computer do what you have programmed it to do. It is the source of programmers' arrogance and impatience with people who are not programmers. If you cannot write a program, you simply do not get it. If you do not get it, how can you possibly control what the programmers do?

The answer is that you cannot. Even so, software developers need and want strong, competent management. They want the manager to do a good job, but not to be overbearing and controlling. They know much that you don't.

To work with programmers as people and not as an abstract resource, you need to understand what they care about, what they value. Gerald Weinberg [Weinberg, 1998] writes, "Managers who pay attention to programmers get good results. . . . Many software development managers simply hate working with their staff, mainly because they have never received any training on how to do that task."

Programmers care about competency, respect, and professionalism. Just as they are scornful of poor managers, they appreciate good managers. In their minds, their job is to write good code; managers take responsibility for the success of the projects and the organization. You can develop a partnership with your developers by doing your job, effectively looking after the project as a whole, sharing the effort in making plans and commitments, and trusting the programmers with the technical work.

The Social Contract   The formal contract between an employer and an employee consists of signed papers and labor laws. There is also a social contract between managers and employees that establishes how they will interact and what each can expect from the other.

- **The old approach.** The manager says, "Do what I say and I'll pay you. I'm the boss; you're the peon. Since you do what I say, you share no responsibility for the success of the project. Your responsibility ends with doing my bidding."

- **The new approach.** The manager says, "I'll share the vision of success, give you a role to play on the team, and provide you with the tools, the time, the teammates, and the autonomy to achieve success. Rather than giving you detailed assignments, I will stay involved so we can share responsibility for success."

It is easy to see why some managers and staff prefer the old approach. Managers are given the illusion of control while employees take comfort that they do not have to think too hard; all that is required is that they do their job. The old approach suggests a mechanistic, assembly-line policy. Some of the more enlightened readers may be surprised how prevalent the old approach is in the field.

The new approach, which places more responsibility on the workers and requires more leadership from the managers, is consistent with a modern, collaborative strategy. Experience, as well as theory, has verified the superiority of the new social contract. We started implementing it at IBM in the early 1990s.

The social contract between the manager and the employee can be formalized in the employee's performance plan. Performance goals and appraisals should be restricted to three topics:

1. Individual contributions towards project success: the quality of each individual's deliverables and success in meeting commitments

2. Collaboration success: the value of contributions to other members' work; ability to maintain constructive relationships; success in cross-team negotiations and issue resolution

3. Professional growth: what he or she did to build new, relevant skills

These appraisal areas are sufficient to reinforce the desired individual behavior under the new approach.

6.2.5 Adjusting to Team Personalities

The best management training provides the manager with a variety of tools for dealing with individuals and teams. It also helps the manager understand when to apply the tools. For example, an experienced employee may need support to facilitate his or her work while an inexperienced employee may simply need direction. The effective leader provides direction in some situations and drives consensus in others.

The same reasoning applies to teams. A team with enough communications freedom for order to emerge will seem to have a team personality. This personality may or may not be appropriate to the development. Some teams can envision great ideas but seem to lose interest when it comes time to deliver. Others only seem capable of following specific directions and come to a halt while waiting to be told what to do next. The manager must evaluate the team and decide what style is appropriate. For example, it may be possible to lead an experienced team working within their comfort zone by consensus. A team facing greater challenges may need the manager to be more involved. In such situations, you can choose to play a team member role or, for the short term, to serve as a commander giving orders.

6.2.6 Walking the Walk

To succeed in enabling order to emerge from an unpredictable system, it is critical to "walk the walk" and not just "talk the talk." You must carry out your role in the process without usurping other roles. If a staff member is not doing an effective job and is putting the project at risk, counsel, train, or replace him or her, but do not do his or her work. When you step in and do a staff member's work, you upset the order and foster chaos.

You cannot expect a team to adopt a process that you do not follow. In particular,

- The manager must manage at the appropriate level of detail, remaining focused on the bigger picture.

- The manager must be comfortable reviewing work in progress, not only finished products. The issue here is trust.

- The manager must demonstrate an understanding of team processes and progress. This too is a trust issue.

6.3 COMMITMENT AND BUY-IN

All the concepts in this chapter come down to one factor: the ability of you and your team to make and meet a commitment to execute a development plan. As a leader, you must represent your team in committing to the business or customer that you will solve the development problem, which is to deliver the required software within the given budget and schedule. The dilemma of software development is that sufficient information to reach a level of certainty in making the firm commitment required by the business is often lacking, yet that commitment is essential for the business to proceed. Customers, marketing, and business planning need to know well in advance when a product will be available. In some cases, the company's price may depend on a successful delivery of the system to market. The manager is called on to make a firm commitment without a firm foundation.

Conflict exists in performing this balancing act. Different stakeholders have different interests. The team wants a reasonably low-risk schedule and budget; the business will push toward a tighter schedule and budget. The software manager is caught in the middle. Because any plan is at best an estimate, there is no single, easy way to reach a perfect compromise, but it must be done. This is why the software function is so problematic for a business.

The software manager must proceed by attaining the best possible estimates, assessing the flexibility in the plan, determining how much risk can reasonably be assumed, facilitating buy-in to the plan, and doing everything possible to promote efficiency.

6.3.1 Estimation

In order to make a development commitment, you need to have the best information possible about the size of the effort, the programmer-months, and the schedule required to deliver. One of the truisms of software development is that the estimates are never very good.

The actual budget for a given development project always carries some uncertainty. Consider the software development economics model in Chapter 4. Recall, its predictions were within 30% of the actual values for roughly 80% of the projects. Some believe that more predictability is possible by "calibrating the organization," that is, by making a series of estimates, tracking those against experience, and then adjusting various parameters to improve predictability for your organization. Even though some improvement might result from all of that effort, I am skeptical that there will much payoff. Generally, 30% uncertainty is the best one should expect, given the inherent uncertainty of nonlinear systems.

Even so, estimation tools are worth using as long as the result is used intelligently. The tools can help make the tradeoffs between cost and schedule. Remember that adding staff to accelerate a schedule adds inefficiencies and will probably result in more cost. For example, doubling the staff may only reduce the duration of the effort by 20% but will double the cost.

Several tools purport to provide a good estimate of the time and effort of a project; all have limitations. Some tools use the requirements as input; some use an analysis of the top-level logical architecture. The tools based on requirements assume the architecture, such as client-server, and can work if the project uses that architecture. I prefer Boehm's COCOMO post-architecture model [Boehm, 2000]. Although this model requires an initial view of the architecture and therefore takes more analysis than the requirements-based tools, it gives more reliable answers.

6.3.2 Balancing Risk and Flexibility

As a manager, you must decide how much risk you will assume. Four variables must be balanced: cost, schedule, quality, and content. Once you commit to a plan, cost and schedule are more or less fixed. When committing to a plan, you must determine whether there is enough flexibility to account for the uncertainty.

Compromising quality is tempting, but it is cheating. In the long run, compromising quality will usually cost the business more than a slip in schedule or a budget overrun. Some very successful software companies compromise and push a product out the door in order to make a market window. Presumably, they have balanced service costs with loss of market opportunity. Because software license agreements entail little liability by the producer, this can be a reasonable business decision. However, I do not recommend committing to a plan based on the assumption that quality is an option.

6.3.3 Whose Plan Is It?

The project plan can be viewed several different ways, depending on whose plan it is.

- Their plan. In some organizations, business development or marketing develops the project plan and hands it to the project manager for implementation. It is their plan, and the project manger is expected to deliver. It is little wonder that most such plans are not successfully met. Those who set the plan are only interested in the business and have no responsibility for delivery. They make promises the manager cannot keep.

- Your plan. It is no better for the project manager to set the project plan and impose it on the team. When the content, cost, and schedule are simply handed to the team, they may not commit to them. They see it as your plan and not theirs. Starting a project on this note is a sure way to limit your involvement and the first big step toward the old social contract.

- The team's plan. Another possibility is for the project manager to ask the team to develop the project plan, and then hold them strictly to it. Or the manager may help the team develop the plan through a consensus process. This will be the team's plan, which is an improvement. The team is more likely to commit to the plan if they believe it is achievable. If it is achievable but hard to meet, it is important that team buy-in be a part of the process. The problem with this approach is that it distances the manager from the team. The manager surrenders the opportunity to become involved and to influence the outcome.

- Our plan. This is the best and only acceptable answer, as well as the hardest to achieve. It benefits no one to accept an unreasonable plan from above or an inadequate plan from below. All stakeholders must agree that the plan is acceptable. Everyone involved must believe that their concerns have been addressed and the best balance of content, cost, and schedule has been met. For this to happen, the project manager and the team must work together to develop the estimations of cost and schedule for a given content, discussing the tradeoffs and sharing in the agreements. The manager may sell but does not proscribe. The manager must also work with the other stakeholders to understand the priority of content and the flexibility in cost and schedule. This resulting project plan and the underlying assumptions must be reviewed continually with all interested parties. Achieving the "our plan" situation is the best step toward being a constructively involved leader.

6.3.4 Meeting Commitments

It is useful to approach any estimate of cost or schedule statistically. The higher the budget and the longer the schedule, the lower the likelihood of failure. Conversely, smaller budgets and shorter durations have higher risk. Business needs lead to a paradox that must be addressed by the manager: The business requires the project to assume a risky plan, but not failure.

The answer lies in the nature of the commitment; what are you committing to? If you are committing to setting a plan and then meeting that initial plan without change, you will most likely fail. If you commit to a solution of the development problem, meeting stakeholders' needs within a given schedule and budget, you have a chance of success. The way to meet this commitment is to use the estimation tools to get a ballpark figure, back off the estimates to give yourself as much leeway as the business situation will allow, and then apply the techniques discussed in the earlier chapters. In particular, take extra care to manage content. Remember, shipping the initially planned content is not what matters; it is shipping the right content to meet all the stakeholders' needs.

6.4 THE FINAL WORD: MODERN LEADERSHIP

When I was struggling with my Ph.D. dissertation in mathematics, I occasionally found myself trying (and failing, fortunately) to prove a false theorem. I realized that one cannot fight reality. Managing software development projects using one of the old-fashioned methods ignores the fundamental nature of the development process. Such an activity is a form of fighting reality and, predictably, produces dismal consequences.

The modern management methods discussed in this book reflect my best understanding of how projects work. Following them is remarkably rewarding; things simply go better. You shake off the sense of futility common with the old methods. Rather than being continually frustrated, you will be effective and your projects will come together. Try it and you will never go back.

TO LEARN MORE

During last few years, several good books on the application of complexity theory to management have appeared. I recommend everyone read these:

- Wheatley, Margaret. *Leadership and the New Science: Discovering Order in a Chaotic World*, Berrett-Kohler Publishers, 1999.

- Lewin, Roger and Birute Regine. *The Soul at Work*, Simon and Schuster, 2000.

- Lissack, Michael and Johan Roos. *The Next Common Sense*, Nicholas Breadley Publishers, 1999.

There is a rich literature on working with software developers. Three classics are

- Constantine, Larry. *Constantine on Peopleware*, Prentice Hall, 1995.

- Demarco, Tom and Timothy Lister. *Peopleware, Productive Projects and Teams* (2nd ed.), Dorset House, 1999.

- Weinberg, Gerald. *The Psychology of Computer Programming* (Anniversary Ed.), Dorset House, 1999.

A more extensive discussion of the project review content may be found in my first book:

- Cantor, Murray. *Object-Oriented Project Management with UML*, John Wiley, 1998.

The following reports are surprisingly interesting reading, making clear the dangers of management by slogan. The first reference blames the Mars Climate Orbiter mishap on project management practices based on the "Faster, Better, Cheaper" approach. The Audit Report reflects the confusion caused by the slogan.

- NASA, *Report on Project Management in NASA by the Mars Climate Orbiter Mishap Board*, March 13, 2000, online at http://www.science.ksc.nasa.gov/mars/msp98/misc/MCO_MIB_Report.pdf

- NASA, *Faster, Better, Cheaper: Policy Strategic Planning and Human Resource Management*, Office of the Inspector General Audit Report, March 13, 2001, online at http://www.hq.nasa.gov/office/oig/hq/ig-01-009.pdf

The COCOMO II model is documented in

- Boehm et al. *Software Cost Estimation with COCOMO II*, Prentice Hall, 2000.

I do not discuss organizational change. There are already excellent books on the subject. I highly recommend

- Kotter, John. *Leading Change*, Harvard Business School Press, 1996.

Three Failed Approaches to Software Development

This appendix describes three common, yet inadequate, approaches to software development leadership.

Prior to the approaches to software development discussed in the body of the book, there were three common approaches to managing software development:

- The waterfall process

- Hands-off approach

- Rapid prototyping

Although each method provides some useful lessons, none of them is based on a full understanding of the special characteristics of software development. Each of them is flawed.

I am not aware of any authors who currently promote these approaches, yet they are currently practiced. You may recognize the approach in your organization. If so, by the end of this appendix, you should have a basis for understanding why your organization may have found software development particularly troubling.

There is much at stake. If you blindly practice any one of these approaches, you could do a lot of harm to yourself and your organization. No matter how well intentioned you are, choosing the wrong approach to software development adds risk and expense to projects. Your organization will ultimately be less competitive and will have trouble retaining the best people.

A.1 SOME MISLEADING ANALOGIES

Most of us like to approach new things by asking how they are like familiar things. If we can understand the similarities, then we can apply the understanding of the familiar discipline to the new. It is tempting to approach software development as analogous to other kinds of development processes. In order to be effective as a leader, it is important to choose the right analogy.

For example, if your firm manufactures items, you might be tempted to approach software development as an extension of your manufacturing process. However, manufacturing focuses on developing highly efficient processes for producing many identical items. In software, the only similar problem is creating the distribution media such as the CD-ROMs. Software code consists of thousands or even millions of different items, code fragments such as class specifications, each of which needs to work in concert with the others. Developing these numerous items is a very different problem than is found in manufacturing. Not surprisingly then, manufacturing-based management techniques do not transfer well to software since they address a different problem.

Others note that software development efforts appear to have the attributes of a construction or engineering development project. Like construction, software projects may be thought of as consisting of a set of work items that must be resourced, scheduled, and tracked. However, software and construction are again different entities. In construction, the problem is, given a well-understood design, to identify all of the tasks, assign appropriate resources, identify the constraints and predecessors, and then order the tasks to minimize the critical-path length and/or the budget. In construction projects, there is relatively little discovery of requirements, evolution of design, and content management. Construction-based techniques such as critical-path analysis and Monte-Carlo analysis have limited applicability in software. Software development is more like designing a building than constructing one. Actually, some construction projects, which involve a new design, are much like product development. See Karl Sabbaugh's text, *Skyscraper* [Sabbaugh, 1991].

A.2 THE WATERFALL PROCESS

Software development may seem to have a lot in common with construction or engineering projects, such as building a bridge. A set of activities must be carried out in what seems to be a natural order: requirements gathering, design, building, testing, and finally putting the bridge into general service. From then on, the bridge goes into operation and maintenance. For software, the usual activities are recast as requirements analysis, architecture, design, code and unit test, integration, and system test.

Tasks are serialized in construction projects. For example, you cannot lay the foundation for a building until the excavation is completed and approved. The flooring task must not begin until the joists are inspected and signed off. Early approaches to software development tried to follow the same discipline:

1. The analysis team captured and documented the requirements.

2. When the requirements were approved, the design started.

3. When the design was approved, coding began.

4. Each line of code was inspected. If it was approved, it was allowed to be integrated into the product.

This is the dreaded waterfall process, illustrated in Figure A-1. It was once touted as a way to make software development cost-effective. The thought was that if coding began before the design was approved, some of the coding effort would probably be wasted. In practice, for reasons discussed in this section, the construction mentality inherent in the waterfall process has led to some of the most spectacular software development failures.

Criticism of the waterfall process may seem like beating a dead horse, but reports of its death may be premature. The waterfall process in software development can be likened to a failed process taking vitality from otherwise viable projects. In any case, there are important lessons to be learned from understanding why this approach fails.

Understanding why the waterfall process fails is a critical step to being an effective software manager.

ID	Task Name	Start Date	End Date	Duration	2000 Q4	2001 Q1	Q2	Q3	Q4	2002 Q1	Q2	Q3	Q4	2003 Q1	Q2
1	Requirements	10/24/2000	2/26/2001	90d											
2	Requirements Review	2/27/2001	2/27/2001	0d											
3	Design	2/27/2001	11/5/2001	180d											
4	Design Review	11/6/2001	11/6/2001	0d											
5	Code	11/6/2001	7/15/2002	180d											
6	Test Readiness Review	7/16/2002	7/16/2002	0d											
7	Test and Integration	7/16/2002	11/18/2002	90d											
8	Delivery	11/19/2002	11/19/2002	0d											

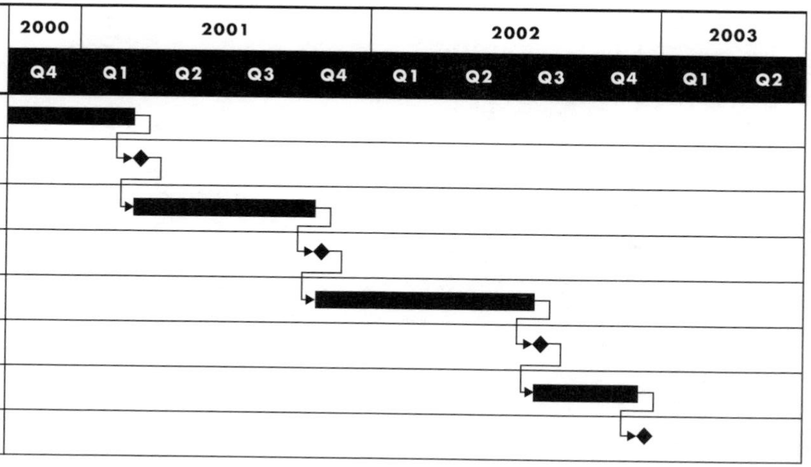

Figure A-1 The Waterfall Process

The waterfall approach includes important disciplines that are useful for all projects:

- Delineating the activities of the development

- Planning for the effort associated with each activity

- Applying the discipline of tracking the progress of activities with milestones

Because these management tasks are obvious elements of any well-managed project, it is a small leap of reason to adopt full-blown classical project management techniques such as critical-path analysis and inchstones. I frequently encounter software managers who are puzzled why such a seemingly effective set of techniques fails in practice.

The first problem with this approach is that the software development tasks are not as easily planned and assessed as those of a construction project. It is simple to know what it means to be half done with painting a bridge. It is difficult to know when you are half done with writing code. The amount of time it takes to paint each part of the bridge is easy to estimate, but no one really knows how large the final code will be, and no one knows exactly how long it will take to write and debug any particular piece of code.

Some managers deal with this uncertainty by demanding precise estimates of progress and time-to-complete. They may point to a Gantt chart, draw a vertical line through today's date, note that the development should be 73% done, and ask whether this objective has been met. The staff may agree, even though they cannot know what they are agreeing to. This process forces the developers to lie to their managers. The outcome is that everything will seem to be on track until the 90% point is reached. Getting to 100% will seem to take forever. Some software development managers may find that efforts are reported as 90% complete for up to 90% of the actual development time.

A second problem is caused by the serialization of the activities: completing one activity before starting the next. To complete an activity implies that the outcome is perfect and that the staff assigned to the activity can move on to the next project, like moving the painters to the next project when they are finished painting the bridge. Although you can tell whether the painting is finished, you cannot be sure whether, say, the requirements document is finished. In fact, experience has shown that you can be sure it is not finished. Over the life of the project, shortfalls in the requirements document will be discovered.

If you try to serialize software development activities, one of two outcomes is likely: early failure or late failure. Successes are rare. Interestingly, the early failures are probably the projects with the most discipline. With the early failures, one of the early milestones, such as the completed requirements specification or design specification documents, is never reached. Each time the documents are reviewed, new problems arise, doubts are raised, gaps are discovered, and questions are asked that cannot be answered. Management is disciplined, insisting on quality and holding to standards. They want flawless documents that describe inhumanly complex systems. Their expectations cannot be met and, in the end, a lot of money is spent with no useful results. There is plenty of blame to go around.

A Colossal Failure

The Internal Revenue Service (IRS) Integrated Case Processing (ICP) systems development effort, from 1993 through 1996, is one example of a failure that used the waterfall approach [General Accounting Office, GAO, 1997]. The IRS estimated that $150 million was spent on ICP from 1993 to 1995, and an additional $77 million would be spent through 1996. Despite this sizable investment, cost and benefits remained uncertain because the scheduled rollout of the ICP workstations continued to change, the ICP capabilities had not been finalized, and so on. In this example, the software development managers spent more than $220 million and had little to show for it. In 1997, the IRS started over by creating a modernization blueprint with a focus on business requirements and architectures to effect tax-system modernization. In 1999, the first prime contract was awarded against the blueprint. Let's hope it goes better this time.

Late failure is more common: Projects seem to go along fine until near the end. Early milestones are seemingly met; documents are written and reviewed. In fact, the team and probably the management both know that only the dates are being met, not their intent. The documents are far from adequate to fully describe the requirements or the design. The developers realize that the documents are useless, so they ignore them. When the document writers are assigned to go on to another project, whatever insights they have achieved go with them. The manager reports that everything is on track without any clear basis for knowing whether the schedule can be met.

With the specifications complete, the manager brings on enough programmers to write the code in the time allotted, based on industry and company experience. For example, a standard estimate is that a programmer can be expected to develop 2,000 lines of tested code a year. (The actual number varies wildly.) If 100,000 lines of code are to be developed in one year, the manager assigns 50 programmers. Each developer is assigned a portion of the design specification to implement.

As the developers try to follow the specification, they find problems, some large, some small. If they detect a design flaw, they find there is no one to talk to because the design specification is frozen and the designers have been assigned to another project. The designers are fully occupied, have no time to revisit this project, and may not even remember the design details. The developers give up and build whatever it takes to get the job done. They fill in the gaps or ignore them, improvise, and hope for the best. Each developer does this pretty much in isolation, without a view of the total project. The project design slowly degrades. Despite reviews, subtle design flaws are introduced that do not become evident until late in the project when all the elements are integrated. Because the code is not built as designed, there is no documentation that describes the developed code. The developers blame the designers for these problems. The end result is code that is hard to maintain or extend.

During this time, the marketing team may inform you that, because of market or customer changes, the priorities set six months ago have been overcome by events. They need the code to meet a different set of requirements. As a manager, you have three bad choices.

1. Hold to the process and, if you're lucky, successfully ship a product that does not meet current requirements.

2. Stop everything and start the project over. Reassemble the analysis and rewrite the requirements specification; find the designers and redesign the code. This is a management nightmare. Just moving people around takes weeks. By the time you get back on track, you may have more unwelcome news from marketing.

3. Abandon the project and hope the same thing does not happen to your next project.

If you go forward, eventually all of the code will be written, reviewed, and ready for integration. Developers call this exercise "train-wreck integration." Now everyone has the first real indication of whether the project is going to succeed or fail. The train wreck usually occurs, panic ensues, and heroes try to make things right. Sometimes they succeed; sometimes they fail. In either case, this is a bad experience for everyone concerned.

Almost certainly, the computer will encounter many errors as it tries to process the lines of code into an executable program. Developers describe this situation by saying the build is broken. The errors are collected and reported to the developers, who respond to them. Finally, the code builds, but it does not run. It usually crashes because of some subtle interaction between the code built by different developers or between the code and the system. Once the crash occurs and the cause is discovered and fixed (which typically takes several days), the code is rebuilt and tested, only to crash again later in the execution. The discovery and removal process, repeated many times, is terribly inefficient because the bugs can only be found one at a time. Most of the team has little to do as each bug is corrected, so there is a lot of pressure to turn the bugs around quickly and little time for niceties such as design and documentation. New bugs are often introduced as existing bugs are removed. This process may take weeks, with no apparent progress. Some projects are even abandoned at this stage; management decides that the build is so broken that it is better to throw it away and start over.

If the code finally runs without crashing too often, a lot of testing remains to be done. Does the code work correctly? Is it fast enough? Defects are found and corrected. At this point, no one has a handle on the code design, so every defect correction is an unpredictable one. A new fatal bug may be introduced that leads to a system crash. The defect discovery and correction process may seem interminable. In some cases, defects are introduced at the same rate as they are corrected, so there is no real progress. Again, management has to make a choice: Abandon the project, try again, or push the code out the door. If management decides to ship, they must expect large service expenses and aggravated customers. This, too, is a less than satisfying experience.

A well-known example was American Airlines' project to integrate its reservation system, SABRE, with the reservation systems of Marriott, Hilton, and Budget. The project was abandoned and American Airlines wrote off $165 million in 1992 [Gibbs, 1994]. This scenario is all too typical, and in the end, everyone is unhappy. Software development teams that are managed using the waterfall approach have little time to consider basics like customer satisfaction, reuse, and repeatable processes. No wonder the literature on the waterfall approach is so grim. The good news is that there are alternatives.

Over the past 30 years, we have learned that software development projects are fundamentally different from construction projects and must be managed differently. The waterfall process works well for the latter but poorly for the former, for several reasons:

- The content of software projects is much more volatile.
  In most cases, construction projects have relatively simple content that does not change once the project is under way, such as the number of lanes on a highway or the number of rooms in a building. If the construction project manager allows even small modifications that result in change orders, the changes will be the cause for much concern and may be considered a sign of poor planning or lack of discipline. The expectation is that the content of the project can be fully understood before the contract is let out for bids.
  Software project content is volatile for several reasons.

  - Software is interactive. Software has a lot of behavior; bridges have little. The behavior of an interactive system is harder to specify than the static requirements of a bridge or a tunnel. Consequently, software customers are often unable to specify their needs fully, in sufficient detail, at the beginning of a project.

  - Software requirements specifications are usually incomplete.

  In time, customers may realize they have forgotten some requirements. During a review they may realize that, because of the ambiguity of the requirements, the behavior of the system may meet specifications but it does not meet their needs and must be changed. This situation happens surprisingly often. In today's fast-moving technical environment, the market frequently shifts during development, changing the requirements and the needed content of the system. Project success may hinge on the ability to accommodate changes. Ignoring them may not be a viable option.
  If the highway department asked a construction manager to add a new lane midway through a bridge construction project, a lot of interesting meetings would be held, newspaper articles would be written, and someone might get fired. But changes in content happen all the time in software development.
  The movie *Bugsy* dramatized mobster Bugsy Seigel's management of the construction of the Flamingo Hotel in Las Vegas. Seigel kept changing

the project, adding walls, for example. The resulting schedule and budget overruns so angered his management (Meyer Lansky and colleagues), they had him killed. (They also suspected that he was lining his pockets with their money.) Fortunately, software development managers are not held to the same level of accountability.

• There is an ongoing tradeoff among expense, schedule, and benefit.
Software development may involve new, innovative code. Because it is often impossible to know how long a given feature will take to implement, there is a risk that the feature will prove to be more time-consuming to develop than was anticipated when the project was planned. As a manager, you must constantly decide which features will be in the product release and which will be deferred. As the project progresses, you may decide that some feature that is nice to have, but not essential, is adding too much risk to the project. You may need to save the project by throwing the feature overboard.

     The manager of a construction project may discover that some feature is adding risk. The original estimates may have been incorrect for some reason; for example, unexpected rock in the soil could cause difficulty in excavation. The construction manager rarely has the luxury of deferring the feature. Instead, the schedule slips or the budget increases, or both.

• Software specifications cannot be frozen.
The underlying assumption behind the waterfall process is that it is possible to make the specifications correct. Experience has shown that because of the complexity of software development, the documents are never correct. The customer or the marketing department is rarely able to specify the requirements with sufficient precision and detail to result in a successful development effort. The designers cannot anticipate how all the elements of the software will work together. The one thing you can count on is that the design will have many subtle flaws. No human mind can comprehend how a software program will execute in sufficient detail to get a paper design correct. Reviews and team walkthroughs can help, but they fall short. Complexity will inevitably result in flawed requirements and design.

- Software projects are not effort-driven.
Fred Brooks was the first to point out the differences between software development and construction projects [Brooks, 1995]. He observed that software development does not have a fixed amount of effort, independent of the number of staff. Consider workers painting the hull of a ship. The amount of effort is fixed, conceivably measured in painter-weeks. The more workers you apply to the job, the sooner it is done. As Brooks pointed out, the same reasoning fails when applied to software, as reflected in the title of his book, *The Mythical Man-Month.*

   The need for communications among the workers illustrates the difference. The painters have little to discuss: "You paint here; I'll paint there. Let's meet for a beer after work." With software development, "You code this; I'll code that" does not suffice. Software developers find that because of the complexity of their task, issues arise continually that require ongoing communications. In fact, as more developers are added, there are more opportunities and requirements for communications. Each developer has to be sure the code developed will work with everyone else's. Because the specifications are always flawed, the developers cannot simply work from the documents. Coordination is inevitable. It is as if all the bridge painters had to get together to discuss exactly what area should be painted by whom. The result is that productivity per developer falls as more people are added to the project. Sometimes the surest way to kill a project is to add more workers.

- The risk profile for a software project is different than for construction.
As a construction project comes together, there is less and less risk. Often, most of the risk is in the beginning, with excavation and site preparation. Once the foundation is laid and the frame is up, the contractor has little fear that the plumbing and the air conditioning will not integrate with the rest of the system. The contractor can rely on the blueprint to be valid and the subcontractors to meet the specifications. By contrast, the riskiest part of a software development project is the train-wreck integration at the end, when there is little opportunity to deal with the risk. No one would knowingly take on a project with such a risk profile.

 Tip No sane person would manage a project by moving all the risk to the end.

- The order of operations is not fixed in software development.

  The major problem faced by the construction project manager is the careful planning of the tasks so that the right workers are available at the right time. The order of the tasks is pretty much fixed. The framing cannot begin until the foundation is laid; drywall installation must follow rough plumbing. Careful planning can achieve some overlap. For example, the painters can follow the drywall crew from floor to floor. This sort of careful planning is the hallmark of a successful construction project manager.

  Critical-path analysis rarely captures the essence of software management. The order in which system features are developed is a lot less rigid. This permits more flexibility in the management of content, so content decisions can be made comparatively late in the project. Equally important, the flexibility in the order of tasks enables an iterative approach to project management. This iterative approach is what makes successful software development possible.

- Software artifacts are abstract.

  Construction projects have very concrete features, which makes it possible to measure the percentage of the project that is complete. If the project calls for pouring 1,000 yards of concrete or paving 10 miles of road, it is easy to determine 20% completion. Progress is demonstrable: The manager can examine the paved road.

  Software managers have a greater challenge. No one can be sure how many lines of code will be needed to complete the project. Because this number changes as the development proceeds, this is no way to measure the percent complete. There are, however, some rough but useful methods for measuring progress. They avoid the lines of code dilemma by measuring demonstrable progress. These methods are presented in Chapter 6.

A.2.1 Systems Engineering V Process

A common variant of the waterfall process is derived from the systems engineering discipline. Systems engineering is concerned with designing, specifying, and verifying the implementation of the components of complex systems. It was developed to meet the challenge of building large aerospace systems such as the Space Shuttle and NATO's command and control systems.

These systems are often so large that their development must be distributed to several companies. One firm, the prime contractor, is assigned the overall design and integration of the system. The prime contractor's systems engineers gather and analyze the system requirements, then design the system by decomposing it into a set of subsystems. Often, they consider various decompositions and analyze the tradeoffs among the alternatives. Once the subsystems are determined, the engineers derive the subsystem requirements. Figure A-2 illustrates the systems engineering approach.

The subsystems may be developed by subcontractors, who are obligated by contract to meet the requirements and specifications for the subsystems. The developed subsystems are delivered to the prime contractor for integration into the total system. The prime contractor's systems engineers verify that the subsystems meet their requirements and oversee the integration.

Some software systems are large enough that their development is distributed among multiple companies or among various organizations within the same company. Firms that understand the systems engineering approach may try to apply it to software development.

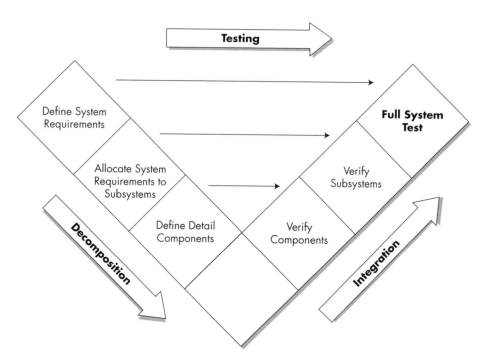

Figure A-2 The Systems Engineering V Process

Initially, the systems engineering approach may seem to be a reasonable approach to developing large software systems. Many systems engineering activities apply to software development:

- Requirements gathering and analysis
- Architecture (identification and specification of the systems)
- Subsystem development
- Integration and verification

However, the systems engineering approach is based on assumptions that do not apply very well to software development: Systems engineering assumes the requirements are stable and the interfaces can be specified adequately before implementation. In practice, the systems engineering approach is a particularly rigid variant of the waterfall approach and its lifecycle, and it inherits all the weaknesses of that approach:

- Classical systems engineering is document driven.
  Systems engineering efforts are driven by formal documents that are developed by engineers and implemented by developers. The problem is that the documents are never correct. The systems engineers rely on their ability to make the document correct. They focus on creating specifications that, once approved, are adequate for determining the design of each subsystem. Any change to the document is managed by a cumbersome change control-board system.

 Tip   A systems engineering approach to software development is driven by inherently flawed documents.

- Integration is late rather than incremental.
  Using the systems engineering approach, subsystems are developed to completion, and then they are integrated at the end of the project. Modern software development calls for ongoing integration of the partially completed subsystems throughout the implementation phase. This ongoing integration accommodates change better and provides a method for managing project risk. This idea is expanded in Chapter 6.

• Relationships are often adversarial.

One key weakness of the systems engineering approach is often a dysfunctional, adversarial relationship between the prime contractor and the subcontracting organizations. Rather than teaming with the objective of achieving a good project, the prime and subcontractors negotiate by contract. The subcontractors are responsible for meeting specifications; they have no responsibility for ensuring that the system works. Flawed specifications are the prime contractor's problem. Ambiguous specifications provide an opportunity for finger pointing and placing blame. When things go wrong, the prime contractor holds out until the subsystem expected is delivered; the subcontractor holds out for more money to account for the scrap and rework caused by the "flawed" specification. Any change in requirements or design is an opportunity to reopen the contract. The late integration only makes things worse. Disagreements may not surface until most of the money has been spent.

You might have noticed that some of the premises underlying software development, such as unstable requirements and evolving design, might apply equally to systems engineering. There are some promising efforts to bring the disciplines together by bringing some of the modern software practices into systems engineering.

A.2.2 Iterated Waterfalls

The founders of software development management, including Winston Royce and Barry Boehm, realized the problems with the classical waterfall process almost from the beginning. In the 1980s, they developed waterfall variants such as the mini-waterfall or Boehm Spiral [Boehm, 1988], which allowed for more customer interaction. These variants broke the development cycle into smaller chunks. Each chunk consisted of a waterfall process in which the requirements were reviewed, the documents updated, and some of the code developed. The output of an iteration served as input to the next. This process of ongoing customer reviews and specification updates made it possible to manage the project risks. Through their insight, pioneers such as Royce and Boehm laid the groundwork for the modern approach to managing software development projects.

A.2.3 Shortcomings

The waterfall approach identifies a project's fundamental activities: requirements management, architecture and design, implementation, test, operations, and maintenance. However, because the nature of software development does not permit requirements and design documents to be frozen, the details of the activities and the artifacts generated for a modern software process are very different from those of a systems engineering project. Consequently, even though we understand that these activities and artifacts must be anticipated, we should not look to systems engineering for their form and content.

Several concepts of the classical waterfall management approach, when suitably modified, are useful to the software manager. The discipline of project planning and tracking is always important. In particular, it is useful to understand work breakdown structures, cost and schedule variances, earned value, and so on. An approach to earned value is discussed in Chapter 6. Critical-path analysis and Monte-Carlo simulation are not very useful.

Does the waterfall approach, which works well for construction management, provide the tools and control points necessary to manage the cost, schedule, and quality risks inherent in software development? The answer is a resounding no. It does not provide the tools the manager needs to control the project. Because the activity-based planning and rigid tasking do not reflect the true nature of the project, it is unlikely the manager will ever have an accurate idea of the true status of the project by assessing the time spent on the activities. Even though the developers can rightly claim that they have completed the activities, the project may be nowhere near completion. Without an accurate view of the status, the manager will not have an opportunity to address the risks early enough to save the project.

As discussed in Chapter 3, the serialization of the activities results in less than optimal use of resources and adds schedule and cost risk. In practice, coding need not follow completion of the design. In fact, some overlapping of coding and design activities is essential. The management approach must recognize this concept.

A fundamental principle of building any large system is that the earlier a manager has insight into a problem, the more likely it can be corrected. The cost of corrections grows dramatically as the project progresses. The waterfall approach of moving integration and testing to the end is folly because it is only at integration that the software development manager has any real indication of the status of the effort. By waiting for the integration, scheduled in the last few weeks of the project, the manager cannot address the four risks while there is still time to take appropriate action.

The waterfall approach also provides little opportunity to address customer satisfaction risk. Experience has shown that when code is shipped, it is very unlikely that the customers will use it. The problem is that much time will have elapsed since the requirements were gathered, and customer needs may have changed. The waterfall approach makes no provisions for customer feedback and iterations that enhance the probability of customer satisfaction.

Finally, there is no practical way to address quality. Managers strive for perfect specifications, then for strict adherence of the code to the specifications. They and their teams become caught up in unending reviews and quality assurance activities. They eventually find they have spent an unreasonable amount of money without ever achieving perfection. For reasons described earlier, such exercises are futile.

Some of the more spectacular large-system failures have resulted from using the waterfall approach. In some cases, millions of dollars were spent trying to get the specifications correct, only to have the customer or sponsor run out of patience and cancel the effort. In other cases, managers have declared a system complete, even though they knew it was flawed. Because there are no provisions for updating the specifications as the system is developed, the waterfall approach inevitably results in the code not being well documented by the specifications. The code is not built as designed. Often there is such a scramble to fix the code during integration and testing, at the end of the project, that the shipped code is hacked together with no consideration of quality.

One underlying problem with the waterfall approach, and the systems engineering variant, is that they do not account for how humans deal with software development problems. These methods force the developers into rigid, inhuman behavior. A successful management approach must take into account the human aspects of software development discussed in Chapter 6.

The systems engineering approach, which is clearly too bureaucratic for small software systems, may seem applicable to large software systems. Even for large systems, however, the systems engineering approach has all the same flaws as the waterfall approach. In fact, because of its rigid reliance on inherently flawed documents and the lack of iterations, the systems engineering approach is a variant of the waterfall approach, at its worst.

The best approach provides management control and oversight while facilitating how developers do their jobs.

A.3 HANDS-OFF APPROACH

Some managers throw in the towel in response to the failures of the waterfall and systems engineering approaches. They observe that methods that produce success in other fields fail in software development. They conclude it is impossible to manage software development, so they do not even try. Believing that strong leadership is all that's needed, their mantra is "Just manage the people."

The weakness in this approach is obvious: If you do not know much about programming and you have no management processes, how will you lead? How will you lead without having a valid approach?

Competent programmers have unique skills and knowledge, like machinists, plumbers, and electricians. Some experienced programmers are like master craftsmen: They apply their years of experience and insight to solve the programming problem at hand by instantly grasping which of their arcane techniques should be applied to a given situation. They know about doubly linked lists, multiple arrays, function pointers, transaction models, Java beans, polymorphism, the difference between aggregation by reference and aggregation by value, interrupts, and so on. In short, they know important material that you do not know and never will.

Given their past failures with process and faced with their inability to program, some managers believe they have no role in managing programmers other than providing the needed tools and environment, obtaining agreement as to what needs to be done (an often painful process), and getting out of the way. The underlying principle is to establish a trusting relationship with the software developers and hope for the best.

This is how some construction bosses manage electricians: They hire an electrician to do a job, and they have little influence on how the job is done. Because electricians do not take well to oversight, a wise construction boss does everything possible to develop a good relationship with the electrician in the hope that establishing a good rapport will result in a good job finished on time. Managers who advocate this approach may consider their lack of involvement or oversight a virtue. They "trust their people."

Tip Programming is a craft, but that does not mean programmers should be managed like craftsmen.

Trust is no substitute for management. On a recent flight I sat next to a fellow who is responsible for setting up the project control infrastructure at a major aerospace firm. I was not surprised when he told me that his organization does not collect and track project development metrics. He said that most of the second-level managers could not be bothered; they trust their people and just want to be kept informed about the big picture. The third-level managers find this frustrating, however, and wish they had better data.

I asked, "Does your company have a factory?" "Yes," he answered. I pressed on, "Do any of the factory managers run their departments without collecting data?" "Of course not. Anyone who tried that would be fired." "But," I asked, "don't those managers trust their people?" "Of course," he answered.

Developing software is different than assembling items in a factory, not because the factory workers are less trustworthy than developers, but because factory operation has become a mature discipline over the past 100 years, with well-understood, fine-tuned processes. Every factory manager is expected to understand process automation, inventory control, supply chain management, quality control, operations research, and so on.

We have been developing software for only about 35 years. Although software development processes are not as mature or well understood as the processes involved in manufacturing, enough is known to give the manager plenty of opportunity to make a critical difference. Although you respect your staff as professionals, you must still provide leadership, direction, and oversight.

The days of the hero programmer, the lone hacker, are pretty much gone. Modern software development is a team activity. Teams consist of a wide range of roles and skills: system architects, programmers, user-interface designers, database designers, product configuration managers, test planners, and system testers. Teams of more than a handful of people do not mesh without leadership. I have assessed many projects headed by uninvolved managers. The primary complaint by the developers is that they do not know what their job is. Without leadership, the organization never develops enough structure for the team to operate. Believe it or not, your team really appreciates the right level of management involvement because they need effective leadership.

Software projects are volatile; they are often bombarded with new or changing requirements. Upper management may reset priorities with each customer call. Without a disciplined leader who sets the course, the direction of software projects may fluctuate wildly. Every day or so, the project could be headed in a different direction. Programmers may become resentful, believing (correctly) that their time and talents are being wasted. The software manager must filter external inputs to the project so that only essential changes are worked. This keeps the project on course while still meeting business objectives.

Software projects are also risky: Content can change, estimates can be wrong, and so on. Without the proper oversight procedures, there is no way to obtain an accurate view of project progress and stability so that the risks can be addressed as they emerge. Unless you and your project managers stay involved in the development activities, your organization will be doomed to a sequence of heroic projects.

A manager who has not been involved will not be able to sort out what worked and what did not. In the absence of planning, discipline, and oversight, it will be impossible to know for sure what contributed to the success or the failure, which also means that there will be little opportunity for organization improvement. Your team will suffer personally and professionally.

Is Software a Science?

Computer science is taught in universities, and the field of software development has benefited greatly from the attention it has received from the academic community. Some people are tempted to expect software development to be as precise and predictable as other scientific disciplines.

Computer science shows there is no way to get precise answers to many questions you might want to ask. There is no rigorous formula for determining the size of the code required to carry out a given task. There is no practical way to prove whether a piece of code is correct, that is, whether it does what it is supposed to do, or even whether the code will stop in a finite length of time. Although there are useful methods for estimating the effort required to develop code, the formulas are based on imprecise parameters and human judgment. Finally, there is no widely accepted formula for code quality, only indicators.

Does the hands-off approach provide the tools and control points necessary to manage the cost, schedule, and quality risks inherent in software development? Unlike the waterfall and systems engineering approaches, the hands-off approach does not impose a structure that adds risk to the development. Because it imposes no process, it neither enhances nor diminishes the manager's ability to address the risks, compared with doing nothing. It provides no mechanism for addressing the risks other than trust. If you adopt this approach, I wish you luck. You'll need it.

A.4 RAPID PROTOTYPING

Rapid prototyping is another response to the failures of the waterfall approach. Frustrated with the rigidity of the waterfall method, some software development pioneers went to the other extreme. They said, "Forget all of those useless requirements and design documents; they are never correct. Just go build the code." Some buzzwords for this approach are *joint application development*, which emphasizes the customer's participation in the process, and *rapid application development.*

Here is how rapid prototyping works. The team talks to the customer about the project requirements. Over a short time period, such as four to six weeks, the team builds a prototype based on their understanding of those requirements. Each time period is called a time box. The team reviews the prototype with the customer and records the customer's reactions. The customer may realize that the prototype requires modification to meet his or her needs. Having examined the prototype, the team should be able to refine their requirements, providing detailed input. The customer may say, for example, that the interface needs to be changed or the reports created by the program have the wrong format. Based on this input, the prototype is adjusted over the next few weeks. Errors are corrected, and more functionality is added. The resulting software is again reviewed with the customer. The process continues until the customer agrees that the product is satisfactory.

It is easy to see why this approach is attractive. Anything that focuses the team's attention onto the customer and the product is a good thing. The approach offers additional benefits:

- The team is highly productive.
  The team's time is spent generating the software rather than generating a lot of specifications that may never be read by anyone and will be obsolete the day after they are developed. Modern development environments such as graphical user interface builders, Java toolkits, and object design and management tools provide the productivity to support the level of interaction required by rapid prototyping. These days it is more efficient to iterate on the code than to try to get the specifications correct. In addition to feedback from the customer, your team will spend little time working from a wrong set of assumptions. This benefit is most evident early in the project. You may end up with working code in a matter of weeks.

 Tip These days it is more efficient to iterate on the code than to try to get the specifications correct.

- The customer interaction is constructive.
  Coming to closure on exactly what a software program is supposed to do is a difficult problem. The customer may not have a clear idea of what is required

until well into the development. Consequently, proponents of this process say, "Why write specifications? We'll elicit the requirements as we go."

Although the rapid prototyping approach offers many benefits, some drawbacks limit its applicability:

- In rapid prototyping, it is difficult to bring the project to closure.
  Because the customer provides continual feedback, an exit condition may never be reached. At each iteration, the customer and team can and likely will come up with another good idea, another must-have. Continual elicitation brings a continual influx of new or modified requirements. The process often runs as an open loop and spirals out of control. The customer may never be satisfied and the project may never end. It takes a lot of leadership to manage a project to closure using the rapid prototyping approach.

- Rapid prototyping is difficult to plan and budget.
  This concern is strongly related to the previous one. If a project is difficult to close, it is difficult to be confident as to its schedule and budget. Rapid prototyping projects are planned around time boxes; each project has a given number of time boxes. Because each time box has the same set of activities, there is no way to predict how many time boxes it will take to finish.

- Rapid prototyping is unsuitable for software developments by large teams.
  It is easy to imagine that this method could work nicely for a small group of developers working with a single customer. It is harder to see how it would apply to a large integrated system involving hundreds of developers.

- The outcome of rapid prototyping may be nothing but a prototype.
  Using rapid prototyping, development of a polished, robust, maintainable, extendible, architecture-based software system is possible, but, I think, unlikely. Rapid prototyping focuses primarily on functionality. The time boxes will almost certainly be spent refining the functionality; there is no time for anything else. In the end, the code may have the right features and interfaces, but it would never be ready for wide distribution or field deployment.

  Although the rapid prototyping method is great for building prototypes, it does not work as well for developing fielded projects. Although it is important to receive and respond to customer feedback, it is a challenge to a project manager to bring the effort to a successful conclusion. My experience shows there is a strong likelihood that this model will result in an infinite loop.

Rapid prototyping fails to address cost and schedule risk. This approach, blindly applied, places no bounds on project cost or completion date. I have seen teams that are developing commercial projects try this approach, only to evolve versions endlessly, never shipping the product.

Rapid prototyping, an example of an *evolutionary model*, has limited utility. If cost and schedule are not concerns, the evolutionary variant might be appropriate. Consider the example of a team developing tools for use within their own company. The team's budget is constant from year to year and not directly tied to delivery. Each customer release is deployed. This team should consider an evolutionary variant as a way to reduce the turnaround time required to respond to customer feedback. Even so, a configuration management process for prioritizing features and changes is necessary.

What Is Spiral Development?

Spiral development seems to mean different things to different development groups. Some managers use the term to mean rapid prototyping; others mean "not waterfall," without specifying any clearly defined process.

The term originates with Barry Boehm, who provided a detailed specification of the spiral model [Boehm, 1988]. He defined it as an iterated waterfall in which each iteration provides increasing software capability. His detailed spiral model is not the informal process most managers describe as spiral.

Even though it is unlikely that anyone follows the Boehm spiral these days, his paper was very influential, and many of the concepts discussed in his book are in practice today.

A.5 INDUSTRY LESSONS LEARNED

Experience with the software development approaches discussed here has resulted in some important lessons for the entire industry. These hard-won insights are valuable in their own right and worth repeating. If you understand and follow them, you will be a better leader of your organization.

- The activity-based project management approach (such as the waterfall method) to planning and execution of projects does not apply to software. Even so, software projects can be planned and managed with discipline.

- The waterfall approach should be abandoned in favor of an iterative methodology.

- Team and customer communications should be the focus.

- Change must be planned for and managed.

- Trust is not a management technique. Success requires involved, competent, informed management.

- Early and ongoing customer involvement is vital. Prototyping is an essential development activity.

- Understanding how your developers do their work and adopting an approach that facilitates their efforts are vital to success. This, of course, is the subject of the main chapters of the book.

To Learn More

I cite this book throughout the text. It is still a must read.

- Brooks, Fredrick, P., Jr. *The Mythical Man-Month* (Anniversary ed.), Addison-Wesley, 1995.

This text, outlining how a skyscraper in New York is planned, architected, and built, shows that even major construction is iterative and not waterfall.

- Sabbaugh, Karl. *Skyscraper: The Making of a Building*, Penguin, 1991.

This is the original article on spiral development. I cite it mainly for historical interest.

- Boehm, Barry. "A Spiral Model of Software Development and Enhancement," *IEEE Computer*, May 1988.

This report delineates the the effort and results of the IRS Integrated Case Processing Effort.

- General Accounting Office (GAO). Letter Report GAO/GGD/ AIMD-97-31, January 17, 1997.

This watershed paper is often cited as an authoritative view of the state of the industry. It is a bit dated and, in my opinion, overly pessimistic.

- Gibbs, W. Wayt. "Software's Chronic Crisis," *Scientific American,* September 1994.

Here are two references on the systems engineering development approach.

- Blanchard, Benjamin and Wolter J. Fabrycky. *Systems Engineering and Analysis* (3rd ed.), Prentice Hall, 1998.
- Lacy, James A. *Systems Engineering Management,* McGraw-Hill, 1992 (reprinted by the author, 1994).

Bibliography

Air Force, Dept. of. *Software Technology Support Center (STSC), Guidelines for Successful Acquisition and Management of Software-Intensive Systems*, version 2.0, 1996. [ch. 4]

Ambler, Scott and Larry Constantine. *The Unifeld Process Construction Phase: Best Practices in Implementing the UP*, CMP Books, 2000a. [ch. 5]

Ambler, Scott and Larry Constantine. *The Unified Process Inception Phase: Best Practices in Implementing the UP*, CMP Books, 2000b. [ch. 5]

Ambler, Scott, Larry Constantine, and Roger Smith. *The Unified Process Elaboration Phase: Best Practices in Implementing the UP*, CMP Books, 2000. [ch. 5]

Bak, Per. *How Nature Works*, Copernicus, 1999. [ch. 3, 4]

Blanchard, Benjamin and Wolter J. Febrycky. *Systems Engineering and Analysis* (3rd ed.), Prentice Hall, 1998. [appendix]

Boehm, Barry. *Software Engineering Economics*, Prentice Hall, 1981. [ch. 3, 4]

Boehm, Barry. "A Spiral Model of Software Development and Enhancement," *IEEE Computer*, May 1988. [appendix]

Boehm, Barry, et al. *Software Cost Estimation with COCOMO II*, Prentice Hall, 2000. [ch. 3, 4]

Booch, Grady. *Object Solutions: Managing the Object-Oriented Project*, Addison-Wesley, 1996. [ch. 5]

Booch, Grady, James Rumbaugh, and Ivar Jacobson. *The Unified Modeling Language User Guide*, Addison-Wesley, 1999. [ch. 2, 3]

Brooks, Fredrick P., Jr. *The Mythical Man-Month* (Anniversary ed.), Addison-Wesley, 1995. [ch. 3, 4, appendix]

Cantor, Murray. *Object-Oriented Project Management with UML*, John Wiley, 1998. [ch. 5, 6]

Clausing, Donald. *Total Quality Development: A Step-by-Step Guide to World Class Concurrent Engineering*, American Society of Mechanical Engineers, 1994. [ch. 1]

Constantine, Larry. *Constantine on Peopleware*, Prentice Hall, 1995. [ch. 6]

Demarco, Tom and Timothy Lister. *Peopleware, Productive Projects and Teams* (2nd ed.), Dorset House, 1999. [ch. 6]

Douglass, Bruce Powel. *Doing Hard Time: Developing Real-Time Systems with UML, Objects, Frameworks and Patterns*, Addison-Wesley, 1999. [ch. 2]

Eriksson, Hans-Erik and Magnus Penker. *Business Modeling in UML*, John Wiley, 2000. [ch. 2]

Fowler, Martin and Kendall Scott. *UML Distilled: A Brief Guide to the Standard Object Modeling Language*, (2nd ed.) Addison-Wesley, 2000. [ch. 2]

Gibbs, W. Wayt. "Software's Chronic Crisis," *Scientific American*, September 1994. [appendix]

Gorchels, Linda. *The Product Manager's Handbook*, NTC Business Books, 1995. [ch. 3]

General Accounting Office (GAO). Letter Report GAO/GGD/AIMD-97-31, January 17, 1997. [appendix]

Guttman, Michael and Jason R. Matthews. *The Object Revolution*, John Wiley, 1995. [ch. 2]

Harry, Mikel and Richard Schroeder. *Six Sigma, the Breakthrough Management Strategy Revolutionizing the World's Top Corporations*, Doubleday, 1999. [ch. 1]

Herzum, Peter and Oliver Sims. *Business Component Factory*, John Wiley, 2000. [ch. 4]

Jacobson, Ivar, Grady Booch, and James Rumbaugh. *The Unified Software Development Process*, Addison-Wesley, 1999. [ch. 5]

Jacobson, Ivar, Martin Griss, and Patrik Jonsson. *Software Reuses: Architecture, Process, and Organization for Business Success*, Addison-Wesley, 1999. [ch. 2]

Kauffman, Stuart. *At Home in the Universe: The Search for Laws of Self Organization and Complexity*, Oxford University Press, 1996. [ch. 3]

Koch, Richard. *The 80/20 Principle: The Secret of Achieving More with Less*, Bantam Doubleday Dell Publications, 1998. [ch. 4]

Knuth, Donald E. *The Art of Computer Programming: Sorting and Searching*, vol. 3, (2nd ed.), Addison-Wesley, 1998. [ch. 4]

Kotter, John. *Leading Change*, Harvard Business School Press, 1996. [ch. 6]

Kruchten, Philippe. *The Rational Unified Process, An Introduction* (2nd ed.), Addison-Wesley, 2000. [ch. 5]

Lacey, James A. *Systems Engineering Management*, McGraw-Hill, 1992 (reprinted by the author, 1994). [appendix]

Lee, Richard and William Tepfenhart. *UML and C++, A Practical Guide to Object-Oriented Development*, Prentice Hall, 1997. [ch. 2]

Leveson, Nancy G., *Safeware: System Safety and Computers*, Addison-Wesley, 1995. [ch.1]

Lewin, Roger. *Complexity: Life at the Edge of Chaos* (2nd ed.). University of Chicago Press, 1999. [ch. 3]

Lewin, Roger and Birute Regine. *The Soul at Work*, Simon and Schuster, 2000. [ch. 3, 6]

Lissack, Michael and Johan Roos. *The Next Common Sense*, Nicholas Breadley Publishers, 1999. [ch. 6]

Marshall, Chris. *Enterprise Modeling with UML: Designing Successful Software through Business Analysis*, Addison-Wesley, 2000. [ch. 2]

Miller, George A. "The Magical Number Seven, Plus or Minus Two: Some Limits on our Capacity for Processing Information," *Psychological Review, 63*, 81–97, 1956. [ch. 3]

Muller, Robert J. *Database Design for Smarties, Using UML for Data Modeling*, Morgan Kaufman, 1999. [ch. 2]

NASA, *Report on Project Management in NASA by the Mars Climate Orbiter Mishap Board,* March 13, 2000, online at http://science.ksc.nasa.gov/mars/msp98/misc/MCO_MIB_Report.pdf

NASA, *Faster, Better, Cheaper: Policy Stategic Planning and Human Resource Management,* Office of the Inspector General Audit Report, March 13, 2001, online at http://www.hq.nasa.gov/office/oig/hq/ig-01-009.pdf

Page-Jones, Meilir. *Fundamentals of Object-Oriented Design in UML*, Addison-Wesley, 2000. [ch. 2]

Raskin, Jef. *The Humane Interface: New Directions for Designing Interactive Systems,* Addison-Wesley, 2000. [ch. 1]

Royce, Walker. *Software Project Management: A Unified Framework*, Addison-Wesley, 1998. [ch. 4, 5]

Rumbaugh, James, Ivar Jacobson, and Grady Booch. *The Unified Modeling Language Reference Manual*, Addison-Wesley, 1999. [ch. 2]

Sabbaugh, Karl. *Twenty-First Century Jet: The Making and Marketing of the Boeing 377*, Scribner, 1996. [introduction, ch. 3]

Sabbaugh, Karl. *Skyscraper: The Making of a Building,* Penguin, 1991. [ch. 3, appendix]

Szyperski, Clemens. *Component Software: Beyond Object-Oriented Programming*, Addison-Wesley, 1998. [ch. 4]

Tabrizi, Behnam and Rick Walleigh. "Defining Next-Generation Products: An Inside Look," *Harvard Business Review*, November–December, 1997. [ch. 3]

Ulrich, Karl and Steven Eppinger. *Product Design and Development*, McGraw Hill, 2000. [ch. 3]

Weinberg, Gerald. *The Psychology of Computer Programming* (Anniversary ed.), Dorset House, 1999. [ch. 6]

Wheatley, Margaret. *Leadership and the New Science: Discovering Order in a Chaotic World*, Berrett-Kohler Publishers, 1999. [ch. 6]

Wheelright, Steven C. and Kim B. Clark. *Revolutionizing Product Development*, The Free Press, 1992. [ch. 3]

Online References

Accel-Team.Com, Scientific Management. Lessons from Ancient History through the Industrial Revolution, http://www.accel-team.com/scientific/index.html, 2000. [ch. 3]

Object Management Group, www.omg.org [ch. 2]

www.idef.com [ch.2]

Index

A

Abstraction layer, 19
Action item status, 137
Activities, serializing, 80–81
Actors
    basic description of, 33–34
    use case views and, 33–34
Adaptability, 62–63
Adobe Illustrator, 15
Air Force (United States), 81, 96
Airline reservation systems, 5, 158–159
Air traffic control systems, 7–9
American Airlines, 158. *See also* Airline
    reservations systems
Americans with Disabilities Act, 9
Analogies, misleading, 152
Animation software, xxiv
Appraisals, performance, 144–145
Architecture. *See* Software architecture
Artifacts
    basic description of, 90
    productivity and, 90–92
    project reviews and, 136
    Rational Unified Process (RUP) and,
        102–103, 108
    tool environment and, 91–92

Assembly lines, 59–60, 102, 144
AutoCAD, 15
Automated testing, 120, 121
Automation support, 85
Automobiles, xxiv, 14–16, 21, 132, 139
    class packages and, 38–39
    nonlinear systems and, 60–61, 62
    software projects and, 60–61, 62, 66
    subsystems in, 28–29, 38–40
    use cases and, 38–40
Availability, 11, 20–21
    supportability and, 22
    Rational Unified Process (RUP) and,
        116
    use case views and, 35
Avalanches, 73–74

B

Banking systems, 113
Baseline architecture, 84
Beta testing, 111, 120, 121
Big-bang integration, 80, 101
Boehm, Barry, 74, 75, 147, 165, 173
Boeing, xiii, xxiv
Booch, Grady, 97
Bow wave effect, 109–110

Breadth-then-depth principle, 100, 101, 108, 115
Brittle code, 22, 47
Brooks, Frederick P., Jr., 65, 76, 86, 161
Budget(s). *See also* Cost
    cuts, 140–141
    development problem and, 54
    estimating, 146–147
    limitations, determining, 55
    quality by design and, 24–25
    Rational Unified Process (RUP) and, 108
    team leadership and, 131
Bugs. *See also* Defects; Errors
    classification of, 120–121
    Rational Unified Process (RUP) and, 118–120
    Y2K, 6
Bugsy (movie), 159–160
Business
    analysts, 139
    modeling, 64, 111, 112–113
    needs, 18, 148
Buy-in, 146–149

C
C++ (high-level language), 118
CAD/CAM software, xxiv, 7
Capacity, 17–18
Cars. *See* Automobiles
Cash register applications, 43
Cellular telephones, xiii, 17
Change
    evaluation grid, 89
    request trackers, 91, 92
Chaos
    communications and, 65
    constructive involvement and, 135
    edge-of-, systems, 62–63
    theory, 61–62
Checking account systems, 113

Class(es)
    attributes, 35
    components and, 43
    diagrams, 36–38
    object, 84–85
    packages, 38–39
    specifications, 35
COCOMO, 75, 96, 147
Code
    brittle, 22, 47
    delivering functionality with less, 82
    editors, 91
    generation, automating, 93–94
    reuse, 82–85
    repositories, 84
Collaboration diagrams, 41
Commitments, 146–149
Common sense, 58–59
Communications
    automating, 92–93
    channels, managers as filters in, 140
    leadership styles and, 130
    organizing to enable, 132–135
    productivity and, 76, 86, 92
    Rational Unified Process (RUP) and, 99
    software architecture and, 35, 49
    with stakeholders, 85
    teams and, 49, 64–66, 131, 133–135
Compilers, 91
Complexity
    of computers, 142–43
    defeating, with hierarchy, 78–79
    theory, 86
    use of the term, in the software development economics model, 75
Components
    classes and, 43
    customized, 5
    design of, 41–43
    testing, 119

Component view, 32, 41–45, 116–117
Concept(s)
    development phase, of product
        development, 56, 57, 58
    proof-of-, 58
Configurability, 11, 18
Configuration managers, 64, 91
Congress, 8
Consistency, of artifacts, 92
Construction
    management mentality, 80
    phase (RUP), 107, 109–110, 123
Consumer software, 4–5
Contracts, 113–114, 144–145
Cost(s). *See also* Budgets
    benefit tradeoffs, 68
    of ownership, 10
    portability and, 19
    project plans and, 148
    risk, 67–69
    service, 11, 12
    of testing, 120
Creativity, xxiii, 116
Credit card transaction system, xiii
Critical-path analysis, 152, 162, 166
Customer(s)
    hostility toward, by engineers, 16
    as products stakeholders, 4, 9–11
    use of the term, 9
Customization, of software, 5, 10

D
Database(s)
    productivity and, 79, 90, 92
    Rational Unified Process (RUP) and, 117
Debugging. *See also* Bugs; Defects; Errors
    incremental development and, 80
    Rational Unified Process (RUP) and,
        101
    software architecture and, 41

Decomposition, functional, 48
Defect(s). *See also* Bugs; Debugging;
        Testing
    classification of, 120–121
    free systems, 24
    incremental development and, 79–80
    maintainability and, 21–22
    productivity and, 79–80, 87, 91
    software architecture and, 46, 47
    trackers, 91
    use of the term, 21
Demarco, Tom, 141
Deming, Edward, 99
Department of Defense (United States), 5,
        31
Department of Transportation (United
        States), 8
Deployment view, 32, 44–45, 116–117
Descriptor node diagrams, 44–45
Design. *See also* Software architecture
    extendibility and, 18
    portability and, 19
    Rational Unified Process (RUP) and,
        116–118
    relation of quality to, 24–25, 27
    round-trip engineering principle and,
        93–94
    use of the term, 27
Developers. *See also* Development
    responsibilities of, 64
    working with, 142–145
Development. *See also* Developers
    economics model, 74–76
    knowledge, 77
    lessons learned regarding, 173–174
    manufacturing hard goods and,
        xxiii–xxiv
    problem, basic description of, 54–55
    product development and, 55–58
    productivity, 73–86

Development, *continued*
   risk, approaching, 67–69
   three failed approaches to, 151–175
Discovery rate, 121
Disclaimers, 117
Divide-and-conquer approach, 78–79, 87
Documentation
   eliminating extraneous, 85–86
   leadership styles and, 128–129
   minimizing the generation of, 92–93
   as a paradigm for capturing
      information, 90
   productivity and, 85–86, 90, 92–93
   Rational Unified Process (RUP) and,
      116
   vision documents, 56, 114, 115
Domain knowledge, 77
Downtime, by levels of availability,
   20–21
DSR (Display System Replacement),
   7–9

E

Earned value, determining, 137
Ease of use, 7
Economics model, software development,
   86–87
Edge-of-chaos systems, adaptability of,
   62–63. *See also* Chaos
Efficiency. *See also* Productivity
   improving, 86–90
   intuitive interfaces and, 15
   overtime and, 95
   promoting, the role of tools in, 92
Effort
   reducing the size of, 82–84
   simplifying, 78–84
   use of the term, 74–76
80/20 rule, 81, 118
Elaboration phase (RUP), 106–109

E-mail applications, 18
Engineering. *See also* Engineers
   round-trip, 93–94
   systems, V process, 122–165
Engineers. *See also* Engineering
   automobile, 28
   extendibility and, 18
   hostility toward customers by, 16
   process, 103
   software architecture and, 28, 32
Enterprise resource planning (ERP),
   xiii
Enterprise software, 5
Environment knowledge, 77
EPROMs, 3
Equilibrium state, 62–63
ERP (enterprise resource planning), xiii
Error(s). *See also* Bugs; Debugging; Defects
   detection, 49
   reliability and, 19–20
Evolutionary models, 173
Executable architecture, 101
Extendibility, 18, 40, 48
Extraneous material, eliminating,
   85–86

F

Factory managers, xxi
Fail over time, 116
"Faster, Better, Cheaper" strategy, 141
Federal Aviation Administration (United
   States), 7, 8
Filename extensions, 43
Financial status, reviewing, 137. *See also*
   Budgets; Cost
Flexibility, balancing risk with, 147
Function keys, 15, 121
Functional. *See also* Functionality
   decomposition, 48
   requirements, 115

Functionality, 4–6, 13–14. *See also*
    Functional
    code ruse and, 84
    delivering, with less code, 82
    extendibility and, 18
    incremental development and, 79–80
    intuitive interfaces and, 15
    limiting product, 82
    price quality and, 23
    Rational Unified Process (RUP) and,
        102, 108, 119
    software architecture and, 41

G
Gantt charts, 155
Goals, performance, 144–145
Granularity, 67, 115

H
Hackers, 129–130
Hands-off approach, 105, 167–170
Hardware platforms, 19
Help files, 85
Hewlett-Packard, 30
Hiring. *See* Staffing

I
IBM (International Business Machines),
    30, 127, 144
ICON Computing, 30
ICP (Integrated Case Processing), 165
Idiosyncratic specification, 31
Illustrator (Adobe), 15
I-Logix, 30
Inception phase (RUP), 105–106, 108
Incremental development, 79–80, 104. *See
    also* Development
Initial architecture, 108
Innovation, limiting, 77–78
Integrators, 64

Integrity, of data, 90
Intel, 19
Intellectual property, 4, 27, 30, 50
    investors and, 11, 12–13
    Rational Unified Process (RUP) and, 117
    use of the term, 11
Intellicorp, 30
Interfaces
    basic description of, 43
    components and, 43
    failed reuse efforts and, 83–85
    intuitive, 13–14
Investors
    as products stakeholders, 4, 11–12
    use of the term, 11
IRS (Internal Revenue Service), 156
Iterations, 58, 101–105, 127, 137

J
Jacobson, Ivar, 97
Java, 118, 168, 171
Job descriptions, 61
Joint application development, 171
Joint Technical Architecture, 31

K
"Killing trees," use of the term, 85
Knowledge
    acquisition, 56
    development, 77
    domain, 77
    environment, 77
    role, 77
Kotter, John P., xxi
Kruchten, Philippe, 97

L
Labor. *See also* Efficiency; Productivity
    laws, 144
    minimizing, 74–75

Lansky, Meyer, 160

Leadership. *See also* Management;
    Managers
  commitment and, 146–149
  as key for morale, xxv
  management and, 127–149
  model, 149
  quality software and, 1–25
  style, 128–130
  team, 131–146

Less is more, principle of, 66–67

Leveson, Nancy, 24

Liability, for the reliability of software, 10

Licenses, software, 4, 10

Lifecycles, 56–57, 103, 104, 107, 108

Linear development, 59–60, 66

Lines, drawing, 45–46

Linkers, 91

Linux, 19

Lister, Timothy, 141

Logical view, 32, 35–41, 47, 108, 116–117

M

Macintosh, 15

Mainframes, 62

Maintainability, 21–22, 40, 46, 47, 48

Management. *See also* Leadership;
    Management
  scientific, 59
  by slogan, 141
  of success, 141–142

Manager(s). *See also* Leadership; Managers
  being a, 131–132
  "in complete control," 130
  configuration, 64, 91
  constructive involvement of, 135–142
  employees and, contracts between,
    144–145
  extendibility and, 18
  factory, xxi

  as filters, in communications channels,
    140
  professional satisfaction and, xxv–xxvi
  style of, 128–130
  team member, 130
  uninvolved, 129–130

Manufacturing, xxii, xxiii–xxiv, 2
  assembly lines and, 59–60, 102, 144
  recommended reading, 25

Many-to-many relationships, 40

Marketing, 55, 56, 146

Mathematics, 54

MCI Systemhouse, 30

Mead, Kenneth, 8

Mean time between failures (MTBF), 20

Memory, 48

Methods, basic description of, 35

Micromanagement, 123

Microsoft, 3, 15, 30, 45

Milestones, 68, 95
  Rational Unified Process (RUP) and,
    100–101, 103, 108
  waterfall process and, 156

Military projects, xxiv, 5, 31, 81

Modularity, 28–29, 118

Monte-Carlo analysis, 152, 166

Morale, xxv

Mythical man-month dilemma, 76, 86, 161

Mythical Man-Month, The (Brooks), 76

N

NASA (National Aeronautics and Space
    Administration), 140–141

NATCA (National Air Traffic Controllers
    Association), 8–9

NATO (North Atlantic Treaty
    Organization), 162

Needs, imprecise descriptions of, 14

Nonlinear nature, of software projects, 53,
    58–66, 73–74

O

Object(s)
  basic description of, 35, 79
  classes, 84–85
  files, 118
  logical views and, 35–37
  -oriented development, 30, 35–39
  technology, adopting, 79
ObjecTime, 30
OMG (Object Management Group), 30
One-to-one relationships, 40
Oracle, 30
Organization(s). *See also* Teams
  architecture-based, 133–135
  "calibrating," 146
  charts, 132–135
  competitive, xxi–xxii
  improving the efficiency of, 86–90
  successful, xxiv–xxv
Overtime, misusing, 94–95

P

Paradigms, for capturing information, 90
Pareto, Vilfredo, 81
Partitioning systems, 88–89
Patches, product, 10–11, 22
PeopleSoft, 5
Performance. *See also* Efficiency; Productivity
  portability and, 19
  Rational Unified Process (RUP) and, 116
  of software, basic description of, 6–7
Pilot production phase, 56, 57
Platinum, 30
Portability, 19
PowerPoint (Microsoft), 89, 94, 114
Predictability, 61, 62
Price quality, 23–24

Printer design project, 1–5, 11, 15–16, 18, 24–25
Problem solving
  80/20 rule and, 81, 118
  collaborative, 53, 56, 99, 100
  the development problem and, 54–55
  divide-and-conquer approach and, 78–79, 87
  paradigm, 127
  Rational Unified Process (RUP) and, 99, 100, 105, 116, 117
Process(es)
  engineering, 103
  use of the term, in the software development economics model, 75, 76
Product(s). *See also* Product development
  building the right, 88–89
  patches, 10–11, 22
Product development. *See also* Software development
  basic description of, 55–58
  iterations, 58, 101–105, 127, 137
  lifecycles, 56–57, 103, 104, 107, 108
Productivity
  automating tasks and, 90–93
  customer organization and, 10
  eliminating extraneous material and, 85–86
  hiring and, 77
  improving the efficiency of organizations and, 96–90
  incremental development and, 79–80
  leadership styles and, 128
  limiting innovation and, 77–78
  managing project difficulty and, 76–86
  misusing overtime and, 94–95
  object technology and, 79
  price quality and, 23
  round-trip engineering and, 93–94

Productivity, *continued*
    serializing activities and, 80–81
    simplifying effort and, 78–84
    software architecture and, 45
    software economics model and,
        74–76
    supporting user, 7–8
    training and, 77
Progress metrics, 137–138
Project(s). *See also* Project plans
    architects, 63
    basic description of, 53–71
    development risk and, 67–69
    difficulty of, managing, 76–86
    phases of, 58
    requirements analyst, 64
    reviews, 16, 136–139
Project plans, 54, 66–67
    multiple views of, 147–148
    Rational Unified Process (RUP) and,
        100–101, 108
Prototypes, 23, 57
    80/20 rule and, 81
    rapid, 170–173
    Rational Unified Process (RUP) and, 97,
        105
    schedule risk and, 68
Ptech, 30

Q
Quality
    assurance versus testing, 121–122
    attributes, 13–22
    price, 23–24
    Rational Unified Process (RUP) and,
        121–122
    relation of, to design, 24–25, 27
    risk, 67, 68–69
    software architecture as the basis for,
        49–50

R
Rapid
    application development, 171
    prototyping, 170–173
Rational Unified Process (RUP)
    adopting standard processes and, 98–99
    analysis and, 116–118
    bad processes and, 99–102
    basic description of, 97–125
    business modeling and, 112–113
    constructive involvement and, 135–136
    deployment and, 122
    design and, 116–118
    development disciplines and, 111–122
    good processes and, 99–102
    implementation and, 118–119
    improved results from adopting,
        123–124
    iterative development and, 101–104
    managing success and, 142
    phases of, 104–111
    project management and, 122–123
    project reviews and, 136
    requirements management and,
        113–116
    as a single, unified process, 102
    testing and, 119–122
Record systems, for student grades, 14
Recovery plans, 104, 110
Reich, 30
Reliability, 7, 10, 11, 19–20, 48–49
Repairability, 21, 46–47
Report generators, 92
Requirements
    management, 91, 111, 113–116
    managers, 91
    specifications, 33–35
Reservation systems, 5, 158–159
Responsiveness, preserving, 18
Retailing business, xxi, 34–35, 115–116

Reuse, code, 82–85
Risk(s)
    analysis, 67–69
    balancing, with flexibility, 147
    of building the wrong product, 88–89
    cost, 67–69
    development, 67–69
    managing success and, 141
    market, 58
    project reviews and, 136
    quality, 67, 68–69
    Rational Unified Process (RUP) and,
        104
    schedule, 67–69
    technical, 68
Robustness, 98, 99
    basic description of, 6, 15–17
    software architecture and, 40, 47–48
Role knowledge, 77
Royce, Walker, 74, 95–97, 124, 141–142,
    165
Royce, Winston, 104
Rumbaugh, James, 28

S
Sabbagh, Karl, xxiii
SABRE, 158
Safeware (Leveson), 24
Scalability, 17–18
Scale, diseconomy of, 127
Schedules
    cost and, tradeoffs between, 147
    invention of, xxiii–xxiv
    project plans and, 54, 148
    project reviews and, 137
    Rational Unified Process (RUP) and,
        108
    risk, 67–69
    team leadership and, 131
Science, software development as a, 170

Scientific management, 59
Scope, 108, 137
Sequence diagrams, 41–42
Serialization, 80–81, 85, 90, 99, 116
Service
    costs, 11, 12
    releases, 23–24
Silver bullets, 69
Slogans, avoiding, 140–141
Social contracts, 144–145
Softeam, 30
Software architecture. *See also* Design
    basic description of, 27–51
    as the basis for quality, 49–50
    building teams around, 87–88
    frameworks, 29–32
    investing in, 86–87
    organization based on, 133–134
    specifying, 29–32
Software-as-craft approach, 76
Software development. *See also* Developers
    economics model, 74–76
    knowledge, 77
    lessons learned regarding, 173–174
    manufacturing hard goods and,
        xxiii–xxiv
    problem, basic description of, 54–55
    product development and, 55–58
    productivity, 73–86
    risk, approaching, 67–69
    three failed approaches to, 151–175
Software project(s). *See also* Software
      project plans
    architects, 63
    basic description of, 53–71
    development risk and, 67–69
    difficulty of, managing, 76–86
    phases of, 58
    requirements analyst, 64
    reviews, 16, 136–139

Software project plans, 54, 66–67. *See also*
Software projects
multiple views of, 147–148
Rational Unified Process (RUP) and,
100–101, 108
Software Technology Support Center
(STSC), 81
Space Shuttle, 140–141, 162
Spiral development, 102, 173
Stability, 62, 137–138
Staffing, 68, 77, 108
Stakeholders, 23, 33, 58, 148
basic description of, 1, 4–13
documents used to communicate with,
85
productivity and, 85, 88–89, 92–93
quality by design and, 24–25
Rational Unified Process (RUP) and,
107–108, 114, 119
subsystem architecture and,
88–89
Steel business, xxi
Sterling Software, 30
Stress, xxv
Success
collaboration, 144
definition of, xxiv–xxv
managing, 141–142
performance goals and, 144–145
Supplementary requirements,
115–116
Supportability, 21, 22, 47
customers and, 10–11
software architecture and, 46, 47
System(s)
architect, 117
engineering V process, 122–165
functional tests, 119
operational tests, 119

T
Taskon, 30
Tasks, automating, 90–93
Team(s)
building, around subsystem
architecture, 87–88
communications, 49, 64–66, 131,
133–135
as dynamic nonlinear systems, 63–66
leadership, overview of, 131–146
member managers, 130
personalities, adjusting to, 145
roles, 63–66, 77, 103, 131, 132, 135
use of the term, in the software
development economics model,
74–76
Technical risk, 68
Telephones, cellular, xiii, 17
Television commercials, 127–128
Test-case development tools, 91
Testers, responsibilities of, 64
Testing
automated, 120, 121
beta, 111, 120, 121
completion of, 120–121
incremental development and, 79–80
quality assurance versus, 121–122
Rational Unified Process (RUP) and,
101, 107, 110–112, 119–121
reliability and, 19–20
scripts for, 85
software architecture and, 49–50
types of, 119–120
Time-and-motion research, 59
Tool(s)
environment, 90–93
role of, in promoting efficiency, 92
use of the term, in the software
development economics model, 75

Training, 77. *See also* Staffing
Transition phase, 107, 110–111
Twenty-First-Century Jet (Sabbagh), xxiii

U
UML (Unified Modeling Language)
   adopting, 89–90
   basic description of, 28–30
   quality issues addressed by, 45–49
   Rational Unified Process (RUP) and,
      103, 106, 112–113, 116–118
   recommended reading, 50–51
   round-trip engineering principle and,
      93–94
   superiority of, 29–32
   supporting, 89–90
   views, 32–35, 41–45, 47, 108, 116–117
Uninvolved managers, 129–130
Unisys, 30
United States Air Force, 81, 96
United States Department of Defense, 5, 31
United States Department of
   Transportation, 8
Unit tests, 119
Unpredictability, inherent, 127
Usability, 13, 25, 45–46
Use case view, 32, 33–35
User(s)
   availability of software to, 20–21, 22, 35,
      116
   basic description of, 5–6
   productivity support, 7–8

   as product stakeholders, 4, 5–9
   requirements, 6–7
   use of the term, 5

V
Version control, 119
Views, 32–35, 41–45, 47, 108, 116–117
Vision
   documents, 56, 114, 115
   maintaining, 139–140
   Rational Unified Process (RUP) and,
      114, 115

W
"Walking the walk," 145
Wall Street Journal, The, 2
Waterfall development process
   failure of, 59, 153–167
   mechanistic character of, 59
   Rational Unified Process (RUP) and,
      102, 104–105, 108, 116, 124
   serialization and, 81
Weinberg, Gerald, 143
Wheatley, Margaret, 132
Windows (Microsoft), 15, 19, 43

Y
Y2K crisis, 6

Z
Zachman framework, 30
"Zero-defect" trap, 24

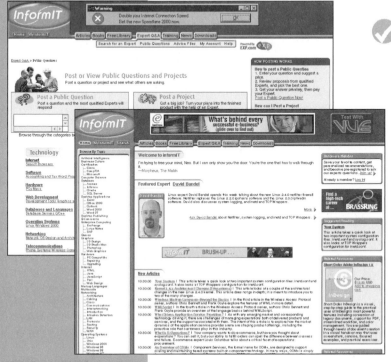